Postcolonialism: A Very Short Introduction

VERY SHORT INTRODUCTIONS are for anyone wanting a stimulating and accessible way into a new subject. They are written by experts, and have been translated into more than 45 different languages.

The series began in 1995, and now covers a wide variety of topics in every discipline. The VSI library currently contains over 650 volumes—a Very Short Introduction to everything from Psychology and Philosophy of Science to American History and Relativity—and continues to grow in every subject area.

Very Short Introductions available now:

ABOLITIONISM Richard S. Newman
THE ABRAHAMIC RELIGIONS
   Charles L. Cohen
ACCOUNTING Christopher Nobes
ADAM SMITH Christopher J. Berry
ADOLESCENCE Peter K. Smith
ADVERTISING Winston Fletcher
AERIAL WARFARE Frank Ledwidge
AESTHETICS Bence Nanay
AFRICAN AMERICAN RELIGION
   Eddie S. Glaude Jr
AFRICAN HISTORY John Parker and
   Richard Rathbone
AFRICAN POLITICS Ian Taylor
AFRICAN RELIGIONS
   Jacob K. Olupona
AGEING Nancy A. Pachana
AGNOSTICISM Robin Le Poidevin
AGRICULTURE Paul Brassley and
   Richard Soffe
ALBERT CAMUS Oliver Gloag
ALEXANDER THE GREAT
   Hugh Bowden
ALGEBRA Peter M. Higgins
AMERICAN BUSINESS HISTORY
   Walter A. Friedman
AMERICAN CULTURAL HISTORY
   Eric Avila
AMERICAN FOREIGN RELATIONS
   Andrew Preston
AMERICAN HISTORY Paul S. Boyer
AMERICAN IMMIGRATION
   David A. Gerber
AMERICAN LEGAL HISTORY
   G. Edward White

AMERICAN NAVAL HISTORY
   Craig L. Symonds
AMERICAN POLITICAL HISTORY
   Donald Critchlow
AMERICAN POLITICAL PARTIES
   AND ELECTIONS L. Sandy Maisel
AMERICAN POLITICS
   Richard M. Valelly
THE AMERICAN PRESIDENCY
   Charles O. Jones
THE AMERICAN REVOLUTION
   Robert J. Allison
AMERICAN SLAVERY
   Heather Andrea Williams
THE AMERICAN WEST Stephen Aron
AMERICAN WOMEN'S HISTORY
   Susan Ware
ANAESTHESIA Aidan O'Donnell
ANALYTIC PHILOSOPHY
   Michael Beaney
ANARCHISM Colin Ward
ANCIENT ASSYRIA Karen Radner
ANCIENT EGYPT Ian Shaw
ANCIENT EGYPTIAN ART AND
   ARCHITECTURE Christina Riggs
ANCIENT GREECE Paul Cartledge
THE ANCIENT NEAR EAST
   Amanda H. Podany
ANCIENT PHILOSOPHY Julia Annas
ANCIENT WARFARE Harry Sidebottom
ANGELS David Albert Jones
ANGLICANISM Mark Chapman
THE ANGLO-SAXON AGE John Blair
ANIMAL BEHAVIOUR
   Tristram D. Wyatt

THE ANIMAL KINGDOM
    Peter Holland
ANIMAL RIGHTS David DeGrazia
THE ANTARCTIC Klaus Dodds
ANTHROPOCENE Erle C. Ellis
ANTISEMITISM Steven Beller
ANXIETY Daniel Freeman and
    Jason Freeman
THE APOCRYPHAL GOSPELS
    Paul Foster
APPLIED MATHEMATICS
    Alain Goriely
ARCHAEOLOGY Paul Bahn
ARCHITECTURE Andrew Ballantyne
ARISTOCRACY William Doyle
ARISTOTLE Jonathan Barnes
ART HISTORY Dana Arnold
ART THEORY Cynthia Freeland
ARTIFICIAL INTELLIGENCE
    Margaret A. Boden
ASIAN AMERICAN HISTORY
    Madeline Y. Hsu
ASTROBIOLOGY David C. Catling
ASTROPHYSICS James Binney
ATHEISM Julian Baggini
THE ATMOSPHERE Paul I. Palmer
AUGUSTINE Henry Chadwick
AUSTRALIA Kenneth Morgan
AUTISM Uta Frith
AUTOBIOGRAPHY Laura Marcus
THE AVANT GARDE David Cottington
THE AZTECS David Carrasco
BABYLONIA Trevor Bryce
BACTERIA Sebastian G. B. Amyes
BANKING John Goddard and
    John O. S. Wilson
BARTHES Jonathan Culler
THE BEATS David Sterritt
BEAUTY Roger Scruton
BEHAVIOURAL ECONOMICS
    Michelle Baddeley
BESTSELLERS John Sutherland
THE BIBLE John Riches
BIBLICAL ARCHAEOLOGY
    Eric H. Cline
BIG DATA Dawn E. Holmes
BIOGEOGRAPHY Mark V. Lomolino
BIOGRAPHY Hermione Lee
BIOMETRICS Michael Fairhurst
BLACK HOLES Katherine Blundell
BLOOD Chris Cooper

THE BLUES Elijah Wald
THE BODY Chris Shilling
THE BOOK OF COMMON PRAYER
    Brian Cummings
THE BOOK OF MORMON
    Terryl Givens
BORDERS Alexander C. Diener and
    Joshua Hagen
THE BRAIN Michael O'Shea
BRANDING Robert Jones
THE BRICS Andrew F. Cooper
THE BRITISH CONSTITUTION
    Martin Loughlin
THE BRITISH EMPIRE Ashley Jackson
BRITISH POLITICS Tony Wright
BUDDHA Michael Carrithers
BUDDHISM Damien Keown
BUDDHIST ETHICS Damien Keown
BYZANTIUM Peter Sarris
C. S. LEWIS James Como
CALVINISM Jon Balserak
CANADA Donald Wright
CANCER Nicholas James
CAPITALISM James Fulcher
CATHOLICISM Gerald O'Collins
CAUSATION Stephen Mumford and
    Rani Lill Anjum
THE CELL Terence Allen and
    Graham Cowling
THE CELTS Barry Cunliffe
CHAOS Leonard Smith
CHARLES DICKENS Jenny Hartley
CHEMISTRY Peter Atkins
CHILD PSYCHOLOGY Usha Goswami
CHILDREN'S LITERATURE
    Kimberley Reynolds
CHINESE LITERATURE Sabina Knight
CHOICE THEORY Michael Allingham
CHRISTIAN ART Beth Williamson
CHRISTIAN ETHICS D. Stephen Long
CHRISTIANITY Linda Woodhead
CIRCADIAN RHYTHMS
    Russell Foster and Leon Kreitzman
CITIZENSHIP Richard Bellamy
CIVIL ENGINEERING
    David Muir Wood
CLASSICAL LITERATURE William Allan
CLASSICAL MYTHOLOGY
    Helen Morales
CLASSICS Mary Beard and
    John Henderson

CLAUSEWITZ Michael Howard
CLIMATE Mark Maslin
CLIMATE CHANGE Mark Maslin
CLINICAL PSYCHOLOGY
    Susan Llewelyn and
    Katie Aafjes-van Doorn
COGNITIVE NEUROSCIENCE
    Richard Passingham
THE COLD WAR Robert McMahon
COLONIAL AMERICA Alan Taylor
COLONIAL LATIN AMERICAN
    LITERATURE Rolena Adorno
COMBINATORICS Robin Wilson
COMEDY Matthew Bevis
COMMUNISM Leslie Holmes
COMPARATIVE LITERATURE
    Ben Hutchinson
COMPLEXITY John H. Holland
THE COMPUTER Darrel Ince
COMPUTER SCIENCE
    Subrata Dasgupta
CONCENTRATION CAMPS Dan Stone
CONFUCIANISM Daniel K. Gardner
THE CONQUISTADORS
    Matthew Restall and
    Felipe Fernández-Armesto
CONSCIENCE Paul Strohm
CONSCIOUSNESS Susan Blackmore
CONTEMPORARY ART
    Julian Stallabrass
CONTEMPORARY FICTION
    Robert Eaglestone
CONTINENTAL PHILOSOPHY
    Simon Critchley
COPERNICUS Owen Gingerich
CORAL REEFS Charles Sheppard
CORPORATE SOCIAL
    RESPONSIBILITY Jeremy Moon
CORRUPTION Leslie Holmes
COSMOLOGY Peter Coles
COUNTRY MUSIC Richard Carlin
CRIME FICTION Richard Bradford
CRIMINAL JUSTICE
    Julian V. Roberts
CRIMINOLOGY Tim Newburn
CRITICAL THEORY
    Stephen Eric Bronner
THE CRUSADES Christopher Tyerman
CRYPTOGRAPHY Fred Piper and
    Sean Murphy
CRYSTALLOGRAPHY A. M. Glazer

THE CULTURAL REVOLUTION
    Richard Curt Kraus
DADA AND SURREALISM
    David Hopkins
DANTE Peter Hainsworth and
    David Robey
DARWIN Jonathan Howard
THE DEAD SEA SCROLLS
    Timothy H. Lim
DECADENCE David Weir
DECOLONIZATION Dane Kennedy
DEMENTIA Kathleen Taylor
DEMOCRACY Bernard Crick
DEMOGRAPHY Sarah Harper
DEPRESSION Jan Scott and
    Mary Jane Tacchi
DERRIDA Simon Glendinning
DESCARTES Tom Sorell
DESERTS Nick Middleton
DESIGN John Heskett
DEVELOPMENT Ian Goldin
DEVELOPMENTAL BIOLOGY
    Lewis Wolpert
THE DEVIL Darren Oldridge
DIASPORA Kevin Kenny
DICTIONARIES Lynda Mugglestone
DINOSAURS David Norman
DIPLOMACY Joseph M. Siracusa
DOCUMENTARY FILM
    Patricia Aufderheide
DREAMING J. Allan Hobson
DRUGS Les Iversen
DRUIDS Barry Cunliffe
DYNASTY Jeroen Duindam
DYSLEXIA Margaret J. Snowling
EARLY MUSIC Thomas Forrest Kelly
THE EARTH Martin Redfern
EARTH SYSTEM SCIENCE Tim Lenton
ECOLOGY Jaboury Ghazoul
ECONOMICS Partha Dasgupta
EDUCATION Gary Thomas
EGYPTIAN MYTH Geraldine Pinch
EIGHTEENTH-CENTURY BRITAIN
    Paul Langford
THE ELEMENTS Philip Ball
ÉMILE ZOLA Brian Nelson
EMOTION Dylan Evans
EMPIRE Stephen Howe
ENERGY SYSTEMS Nick Jenkins
ENGELS Terrell Carver
ENGINEERING David Blockley

THE ENGLISH LANGUAGE
    Simon Horobin
ENGLISH LITERATURE Jonathan Bate
THE ENLIGHTENMENT
    John Robertson
ENTREPRENEURSHIP Paul Westhead
    and Mike Wright
ENVIRONMENTAL ECONOMICS
    Stephen Smith
ENVIRONMENTAL ETHICS
    Robin Attfield
ENVIRONMENTAL LAW
    Elizabeth Fisher
ENVIRONMENTAL POLITICS
    Andrew Dobson
EPICUREANISM Catherine Wilson
EPIDEMIOLOGY Rodolfo Saracci
ETHICS Simon Blackburn
ETHNOMUSICOLOGY Timothy Rice
THE ETRUSCANS Christopher Smith
EUGENICS Philippa Levine
THE EUROPEAN UNION
    Simon Usherwood and John Pinder
EUROPEAN UNION LAW
    Anthony Arnull
EVOLUTION Brian and
    Deborah Charlesworth
EXISTENTIALISM Thomas Flynn
EXPLORATION Stewart A. Weaver
EXTINCTION Paul B. Wignall
THE EYE Michael Land
FAIRY TALE Marina Warner
FAMILY LAW Jonathan Herring
FASCISM Kevin Passmore
FASHION Rebecca Arnold
FEDERALISM Mark J. Rozell
    and Clyde Wilcox
FEMINISM Margaret Walters
FILM Michael Wood
FILM MUSIC Kathryn Kalinak
FILM NOIR James Naremore
FIRE Andrew C. Scott
THE FIRST WORLD WAR
    Michael Howard
FOLK MUSIC Mark Slobin
FOOD John Krebs
FORENSIC PSYCHOLOGY
    David Canter
FORENSIC SCIENCE Jim Fraser
FORESTS Jaboury Ghazoul
FOSSILS Keith Thomson

FOUCAULT Gary Gutting
THE FOUNDING FATHERS
    R. B. Bernstein
FRACTALS Kenneth Falconer
FREE SPEECH Nigel Warburton
FREE WILL Thomas Pink
FREEMASONRY Andreas Önnerfors
FRENCH LITERATURE John D. Lyons
FRENCH PHILOSOPHY
    Stephen Gaukroger and Knox Peden
THE FRENCH REVOLUTION
    William Doyle
FREUD Anthony Storr
FUNDAMENTALISM Malise Ruthven
FUNGI Nicholas P. Money
THE FUTURE Jennifer M. Gidley
GALAXIES John Gribbin
GALILEO Stillman Drake
GAME THEORY Ken Binmore
GANDHI Bhikhu Parekh
GARDEN HISTORY Gordon Campbell
GENES Jonathan Slack
GENIUS Andrew Robinson
GENOMICS John Archibald
GEOFFREY CHAUCER David Wallace
GEOGRAPHY John Matthews and
    David Herbert
GEOLOGY Jan Zalasiewicz
GEOPHYSICS William Lowrie
GEOPOLITICS Klaus Dodds
GEORGE BERNARD SHAW
    Christopher Wixson
GERMAN LITERATURE Nicholas Boyle
GERMAN PHILOSOPHY
    Andrew Bowie
THE GHETTO Bryan Cheyette
GLACIATION David J. A. Evans
GLOBAL CATASTROPHES Bill McGuire
GLOBAL ECONOMIC HISTORY
    Robert C. Allen
GLOBALIZATION Manfred Steger
GOD John Bowker
GOETHE Ritchie Robertson
THE GOTHIC Nick Groom
GOVERNANCE Mark Bevir
GRAVITY Timothy Clifton
THE GREAT DEPRESSION AND
    THE NEW DEAL Eric Rauchway
HABERMAS James Gordon Finlayson
THE HABSBURG EMPIRE
    Martyn Rady

HAPPINESS Daniel M. Haybron
THE HARLEM RENAISSANCE
 Cheryl A. Wall
THE HEBREW BIBLE AS LITERATURE
 Tod Linafelt
HEGEL Peter Singer
HEIDEGGER Michael Inwood
THE HELLENISTIC AGE
 Peter Thonemann
HEREDITY John Waller
HERMENEUTICS Jens Zimmermann
HERODOTUS Jennifer T. Roberts
HIEROGLYPHS Penelope Wilson
HINDUISM Kim Knott
HISTORY John H. Arnold
THE HISTORY OF ASTRONOMY
 Michael Hoskin
THE HISTORY OF CHEMISTRY
 William H. Brock
THE HISTORY OF CHILDHOOD
 James Marten
THE HISTORY OF CINEMA
 Geoffrey Nowell-Smith
THE HISTORY OF LIFE Michael Benton
THE HISTORY OF MATHEMATICS
 Jacqueline Stedall
THE HISTORY OF MEDICINE
 William Bynum
THE HISTORY OF PHYSICS
 J. L. Heilbron
THE HISTORY OF TIME
 Leofranc Holford-Strevens
HIV AND AIDS Alan Whiteside
HOBBES Richard Tuck
HOLLYWOOD Peter Decherney
THE HOLY ROMAN EMPIRE
 Joachim Whaley
HOME Michael Allen Fox
HOMER Barbara Graziosi
HORMONES Martin Luck
HUMAN ANATOMY Leslie Klenerman
HUMAN EVOLUTION Bernard Wood
HUMAN RIGHTS Andrew Clapham
HUMANISM Stephen Law
HUME A. J. Ayer
HUMOUR Noël Carroll
THE ICE AGE Jamie Woodward
IDENTITY Florian Coulmas
IDEOLOGY Michael Freeden
THE IMMUNE SYSTEM
 Paul Klenerman

INDIAN CINEMA
 Ashish Rajadhyaksha
INDIAN PHILOSOPHY Sue Hamilton
THE INDUSTRIAL REVOLUTION
 Robert C. Allen
INFECTIOUS DISEASE Marta L. Wayne
 and Benjamin M. Bolker
INFINITY Ian Stewart
INFORMATION Luciano Floridi
INNOVATION Mark Dodgson and
 David Gann
INTELLECTUAL PROPERTY
 Siva Vaidhyanathan
INTELLIGENCE Ian J. Deary
INTERNATIONAL LAW Vaughan Lowe
INTERNATIONAL MIGRATION
 Khalid Koser
INTERNATIONAL RELATIONS
 Christian Reus-Smit
INTERNATIONAL SECURITY
 Christopher S. Browning
IRAN Ali M. Ansari
ISLAM Malise Ruthven
ISLAMIC HISTORY Adam Silverstein
ISOTOPES Rob Ellam
ITALIAN LITERATURE
 Peter Hainsworth and David Robey
JESUS Richard Bauckham
JEWISH HISTORY David N. Myers
JOURNALISM Ian Hargreaves
JUDAISM Norman Solomon
JUNG Anthony Stevens
KABBALAH Joseph Dan
KAFKA Ritchie Robertson
KANT Roger Scruton
KEYNES Robert Skidelsky
KIERKEGAARD Patrick Gardiner
KNOWLEDGE Jennifer Nagel
THE KORAN Michael Cook
KOREA Michael J. Seth
LAKES Warwick F. Vincent
LANDSCAPE ARCHITECTURE
 Ian H. Thompson
LANDSCAPES AND
 GEOMORPHOLOGY
 Andrew Goudie and Heather Viles
LANGUAGES Stephen R. Anderson
LATE ANTIQUITY Gillian Clark
LAW Raymond Wacks
THE LAWS OF THERMODYNAMICS
 Peter Atkins

LEADERSHIP Keith Grint
LEARNING Mark Haselgrove
LEIBNIZ Maria Rosa Antognazza
LEO TOLSTOY Liza Knapp
LIBERALISM Michael Freeden
LIGHT Ian Walmsley
LINCOLN Allen C. Guelzo
LINGUISTICS Peter Matthews
LITERARY THEORY Jonathan Culler
LOCKE John Dunn
LOGIC Graham Priest
LOVE Ronald de Sousa
MACHIAVELLI Quentin Skinner
MADNESS Andrew Scull
MAGIC Owen Davies
MAGNA CARTA Nicholas Vincent
MAGNETISM Stephen Blundell
MALTHUS Donald Winch
MAMMALS T. S. Kemp
MANAGEMENT John Hendry
MAO Delia Davin
MARINE BIOLOGY Philip V. Mladenov
THE MARQUIS DE SADE John Phillips
MARTIN LUTHER Scott H. Hendrix
MARTYRDOM Jolyon Mitchell
MARX Peter Singer
MATERIALS Christopher Hall
MATHEMATICAL FINANCE
    Mark H. A. Davis
MATHEMATICS Timothy Gowers
MATTER Geoff Cottrell
THE MEANING OF LIFE
    Terry Eagleton
MEASUREMENT David Hand
MEDICAL ETHICS Michael Dunn
    and Tony Hope
MEDICAL LAW Charles Foster
MEDIEVAL BRITAIN John Gillingham
    and Ralph A. Griffiths
MEDIEVAL LITERATURE
    Elaine Treharne
MEDIEVAL PHILOSOPHY
    John Marenbon
MEMORY Jonathan K. Foster
METAPHYSICS Stephen Mumford
METHODISM William J. Abraham
THE MEXICAN REVOLUTION
    Alan Knight
MICHAEL FARADAY
    Frank A. J. L. James
MICROBIOLOGY Nicholas P. Money

MICROECONOMICS Avinash Dixit
MICROSCOPY Terence Allen
THE MIDDLE AGES Miri Rubin
MILITARY JUSTICE Eugene R. Fidell
MILITARY STRATEGY
    Antulio J. Echevarria II
MINERALS David Vaughan
MIRACLES Yujin Nagasawa
MODERN ARCHITECTURE
    Adam Sharr
MODERN ART David Cottington
MODERN BRAZIL Anthony W. Pereira
MODERN CHINA Rana Mitter
MODERN DRAMA
    Kirsten E. Shepherd-Barr
MODERN FRANCE
    Vanessa R. Schwartz
MODERN INDIA Craig Jeffrey
MODERN IRELAND Senia Pašeta
MODERN ITALY Anna Cento Bull
MODERN JAPAN
    Christopher Goto-Jones
MODERN LATIN AMERICAN
    LITERATURE
    Roberto González Echevarría
MODERN WAR Richard English
MODERNISM Christopher Butler
MOLECULAR BIOLOGY Aysha Divan
    and Janice A. Royds
MOLECULES Philip Ball
MONASTICISM Stephen J. Davis
THE MONGOLS Morris Rossabi
MOONS David A. Rothery
MORMONISM
    Richard Lyman Bushman
MOUNTAINS Martin F. Price
MUHAMMAD Jonathan A. C. Brown
MULTICULTURALISM Ali Rattansi
MULTILINGUALISM John C. Maher
MUSIC Nicholas Cook
MYTH Robert A. Segal
NAPOLEON David Bell
THE NAPOLEONIC WARS
    Mike Rapport
NATIONALISM Steven Grosby
NATIVE AMERICAN LITERATURE
    Sean Teuton
NAVIGATION Jim Bennett
NAZI GERMANY Jane Caplan
NELSON MANDELA
    Elleke Boehmer

NEOLIBERALISM Manfred Steger
    and Ravi Roy
NETWORKS Guido Caldarelli and
    Michele Catanzaro
THE NEW TESTAMENT
    Luke Timothy Johnson
THE NEW TESTAMENT AS
    LITERATURE Kyle Keefer
NEWTON Robert Iliffe
NIELS BOHR J. L. Heilbron
NIETZSCHE Michael Tanner
NINETEENTH-CENTURY BRITAIN
    Christopher Harvie and
    H. C. G. Matthew
THE NORMAN CONQUEST
    George Garnett
NORTH AMERICAN INDIANS
    Theda Perdue and Michael D. Green
NORTHERN IRELAND
    Marc Mulholland
NOTHING Frank Close
NUCLEAR PHYSICS Frank Close
NUCLEAR POWER Maxwell Irvine
NUCLEAR WEAPONS
    Joseph M. Siracusa
NUMBER THEORY Robin Wilson
NUMBERS Peter M. Higgins
NUTRITION David A. Bender
OBJECTIVITY Stephen Gaukroger
OCEANS Dorrik Stow
THE OLD TESTAMENT
    Michael D. Coogan
THE ORCHESTRA D. Kern Holoman
ORGANIC CHEMISTRY
    Graham Patrick
ORGANIZATIONS Mary Jo Hatch
ORGANIZED CRIME
    Georgios A. Antonopoulos and
    Georgios Papanicolaou
ORTHODOX CHRISTIANITY
    A. Edward Siecienski
OVID Llewelyn Morgan
PAGANISM Owen Davies
PAIN Rob Boddice
THE PALESTINIAN-ISRAELI
    CONFLICT Martin Bunton
PANDEMICS Christian W. McMillen
PARTICLE PHYSICS Frank Close
PAUL E. P. Sanders
PEACE Oliver P. Richmond
PENTECOSTALISM William K. Kay

PERCEPTION Brian Rogers
THE PERIODIC TABLE Eric R. Scerri
PHILOSOPHICAL METHOD
    Timothy Williamson
PHILOSOPHY Edward Craig
PHILOSOPHY IN THE ISLAMIC
    WORLD Peter Adamson
PHILOSOPHY OF BIOLOGY
    Samir Okasha
PHILOSOPHY OF LAW
    Raymond Wacks
PHILOSOPHY OF SCIENCE
    Samir Okasha
PHILOSOPHY OF RELIGION
    Tim Bayne
PHOTOGRAPHY Steve Edwards
PHYSICAL CHEMISTRY Peter Atkins
PHYSICS Sidney Perkowitz
PILGRIMAGE Ian Reader
PLAGUE Paul Slack
PLANETS David A. Rothery
PLANTS Timothy Walker
PLATE TECTONICS Peter Molnar
PLATO Julia Annas
POETRY Bernard O'Donoghue
POLITICAL PHILOSOPHY David Miller
POLITICS Kenneth Minogue
POPULISM Cas Mudde and
    Cristóbal Rovira Kaltwasser
POSTCOLONIALISM
    Robert J. C. Young
POSTMODERNISM Christopher Butler
POSTSTRUCTURALISM
    Catherine Belsey
POVERTY Philip N. Jefferson
PREHISTORY Chris Gosden
PRESOCRATIC PHILOSOPHY
    Catherine Osborne
PRIVACY Raymond Wacks
PROBABILITY John Haigh
PROGRESSIVISM Walter Nugent
PROHIBITION W. J. Rorabaugh
PROJECTS Andrew Davies
PROTESTANTISM Mark A. Noll
PSYCHIATRY Tom Burns
PSYCHOANALYSIS Daniel Pick
PSYCHOLOGY Gillian Butler and
    Freda McManus
PSYCHOLOGY OF MUSIC
    Elizabeth Hellmuth Margulis
PSYCHOPATHY Essi Viding

PSYCHOTHERAPY Tom Burns and
     Eva Burns-Lundgren
PUBLIC ADMINISTRATION
     Stella Z. Theodoulou and Ravi K. Roy
PUBLIC HEALTH Virginia Berridge
PURITANISM Francis J. Bremer
THE QUAKERS Pink Dandelion
QUANTUM THEORY
     John Polkinghorne
RACISM Ali Rattansi
RADIOACTIVITY Claudio Tuniz
RASTAFARI Ennis B. Edmonds
READING Belinda Jack
THE REAGAN REVOLUTION Gil Troy
REALITY Jan Westerhoff
RECONSTRUCTION Allen C. Guelzo
THE REFORMATION Peter Marshall
RELATIVITY Russell Stannard
RELIGION IN AMERICA Timothy Beal
THE RENAISSANCE Jerry Brotton
RENAISSANCE ART
     Geraldine A. Johnson
RENEWABLE ENERGY Nick Jelley
REPTILES T. S. Kemp
REVOLUTIONS Jack A. Goldstone
RHETORIC Richard Toye
RISK Baruch Fischhoff and John Kadvany
RITUAL Barry Stephenson
RIVERS Nick Middleton
ROBOTICS Alan Winfield
ROCKS Jan Zalasiewicz
ROMAN BRITAIN Peter Salway
THE ROMAN EMPIRE
     Christopher Kelly
THE ROMAN REPUBLIC
     David M. Gwynn
ROMANTICISM Michael Ferber
ROUSSEAU Robert Wokler
RUSSELL A. C. Grayling
THE RUSSIAN ECONOMY
     Richard Connolly
RUSSIAN HISTORY Geoffrey Hosking
RUSSIAN LITERATURE
     Catriona Kelly
THE RUSSIAN REVOLUTION
     S. A. Smith
SAINTS Simon Yarrow
SAVANNAS Peter A. Furley
SCEPTICISM Duncan Pritchard
SCHIZOPHRENIA Chris Frith and
     Eve Johnstone

SCHOPENHAUER
     Christopher Janaway
SCIENCE AND RELIGION
     Thomas Dixon
SCIENCE FICTION David Seed
THE SCIENTIFIC REVOLUTION
     Lawrence M. Principe
SCOTLAND Rab Houston
SECULARISM Andrew Copson
SEXUAL SELECTION Marlene Zuk and
     Leigh W. Simmons
SEXUALITY Véronique Mottier
SHAKESPEARE'S COMEDIES
     Bart van Es
SHAKESPEARE'S SONNETS AND
     POEMS Jonathan F. S. Post
SHAKESPEARE'S TRAGEDIES
     Stanley Wells
SIKHISM Eleanor Nesbitt
THE SILK ROAD James A. Millward
SLANG Jonathon Green
SLEEP Steven W. Lockley and
     Russell G. Foster
SMELL Matthew Cobb
SOCIAL AND CULTURAL
     ANTHROPOLOGY
     John Monaghan and Peter Just
SOCIAL PSYCHOLOGY Richard J. Crisp
SOCIAL WORK Sally Holland and
     Jonathan Scourfield
SOCIALISM Michael Newman
SOCIOLINGUISTICS John Edwards
SOCIOLOGY Steve Bruce
SOCRATES C. C. W. Taylor
SOFT MATTER Tom McLeish
SOUND Mike Goldsmith
SOUTHEAST ASIA James R. Rush
THE SOVIET UNION Stephen Lovell
THE SPANISH CIVIL WAR
     Helen Graham
SPANISH LITERATURE Jo Labanyi
SPINOZA Roger Scruton
SPIRITUALITY Philip Sheldrake
SPORT Mike Cronin
STARS Andrew King
STATISTICS David J. Hand
STEM CELLS Jonathan Slack
STOICISM Brad Inwood
STRUCTURAL ENGINEERING
     David Blockley
STUART BRITAIN John Morrill

THE SUN P. Gordon Judge
SUPERCONDUCTIVITY
   Stephen Blundell
SUPERSTITION Stuart Vyse
SYMMETRY Ian Stewart
SYNAESTHESIA Julia Simner
SYNTHETIC BIOLOGY Jamie A. Davies
SYSTEMS BIOLOGY Eberhard O. Voit
TAXATION Stephen Smith
TEETH Peter S. Ungar
TELESCOPES Geoff Cottrell
TERRORISM Charles Townshend
THEATRE Marvin Carlson
THEOLOGY David F. Ford
THINKING AND REASONING
   Jonathan St B. T. Evans
THOMAS AQUINAS Fergus Kerr
THOUGHT Tim Bayne
TIBETAN BUDDHISM
   Matthew T. Kapstein
TIDES David George Bowers and Emyr
   Martyn Roberts
TOCQUEVILLE Harvey C. Mansfield
TOPOLOGY Richard Earl
TRAGEDY Adrian Poole
TRANSLATION Matthew Reynolds
THE TREATY OF VERSAILLES
   Michael S. Neiberg
TRIGONOMETRY
   Glen Van Brummelen
THE TROJAN WAR Eric H. Cline
TRUST Katherine Hawley
THE TUDORS John Guy
TWENTIETH-CENTURY BRITAIN
   Kenneth O. Morgan
TYPOGRAPHY Paul Luna

THE UNITED NATIONS
   Jussi M. Hanhimäki
UNIVERSITIES AND COLLEGES
   David Palfreyman and Paul Temple
THE U.S. CIVIL WAR Louis P. Masur
THE U.S. CONGRESS Donald A. Ritchie
THE U.S. CONSTITUTION
   David J. Bodenhamer
THE U.S. SUPREME COURT
   Linda Greenhouse
UTILITARIANISM
   Katarzyna de Lazari-Radek
   and Peter Singer
UTOPIANISM Lyman Tower Sargent
VETERINARY SCIENCE James Yeates
THE VIKINGS Julian D. Richards
VIRUSES Dorothy H. Crawford
VOLTAIRE Nicholas Cronk
WAR AND TECHNOLOGY
   Alex Roland
WATER John Finney
WAVES Mike Goldsmith
WEATHER Storm Dunlop
THE WELFARE STATE David Garland
WILLIAM SHAKESPEARE
   Stanley Wells
WITCHCRAFT Malcolm Gaskill
WITTGENSTEIN A. C. Grayling
WORK Stephen Fineman
WORLD MUSIC Philip Bohlman
THE WORLD TRADE
   ORGANIZATION Amrita Narlikar
WORLD WAR II Gerhard L. Weinberg
WRITING AND SCRIPT
   Andrew Robinson
ZIONISM Michael Stanislawski

Available soon:

AMPHIBIANS T. S. Kemp
ENZYMES Paul Engel
VOLCANOES Michael J. Branney and
   Jan Zalasiewicz

WAR AND RELIGION Jolyon Mitchell
   and Joshua Rey
ARBITRATION Thomas Schultz and
   Thomas Grant

For more information visit our website

www.oup.com/vsi/

Robert J. C. Young

POSTCOLONIALISM

A Very Short Introduction
SECOND EDITION

OXFORD
UNIVERSITY PRESS

OXFORD

UNIVERSITY PRESS

Great Clarendon Street, Oxford, OX2 6DP,
United Kingdom

Oxford University Press is a department of the University of Oxford.
It furthers the University's objective of excellence in research, scholarship,
and education by publishing worldwide. Oxford is a registered trade mark of
Oxford University Press in the UK and in certain other countries

First edition published 2003
This edition published 2020

Impression: 4

Published in the United States of America by Oxford University Press
198 Madison Avenue, New York, NY 10016, United States of America

British Library Cataloguing in Publication Data
Data available

Library of Congress Control Number: 2020939202

ISBN 978-0-19-885683-2

Printed and bound by CPI Group (UK) Ltd, Croydon, CR0 4YY

For Yasmine

Contents

Acknowledgements xvii

List of illustrations xix

Introduction: montage 1

1 Subaltern knowledges 12

2 Colonialisms, decolonization, decoloniality 32

3 Slavery, race, caste 41

4 History and power, from below and above 49

5 Nomads, nation-states, borders 61

6 Hybridity 77

7 The ambivalence of the veil 91

8 Gender, queering, and feminism in a postcolonial context 103

9 Globalization from a postcolonial perspective 118

10 Ecology and indigeneity 129

11 Translation 140

References 151

Further reading 159

Index 167

Acknowledgements

Many people have helped me with the writing of this book. For detailed discussion of individual topics, I would particularly like to thank Sahar Sobhi Abdel Hakim, Bashir Abu-Manneh, Sadiq Ahmad, Jeeva and Prathima Anandan, Homi Bhabha, Elleke Boehmer, Tanya Datta, Zia Ghaussy, Indira Ghose, Lucy Graham, Azzedine Haddour, Diana Hinds, Rita Kothari, Neil Lazarus, Roger Little, Matthew Meadows, Paul Mylrea, Parvati Nair, Bernard O'Donoghue, Benita Parry, Ato Quayson, Rob Raeside, Rajeswari Sunder Rajan, Neelam Srivastava, Weimin Tang, Skip Thompson, Megan Vaughan, Joy Wang, Else Vieira. I thank Badral Kaler warmly for her generous support and forbearance, and Maryam, Yasmine, and Isaac for just being themselves.

Acknowledgements to the second edition

In this revised edition I have updated arguments, content, and ideas where appropriate and also, in response to some readers' suggestions, included more theoretical material. I am very grateful to all those who gave me feedback on the first edition. Warm thanks to Jenny Nugee at OUP for inviting me to prepare an updated edition, and to Elleke Boehmer for once again providing detailed and productive input. Yasmine Young provided searching questions early on which were transformative. I thank again all those mentioned above who continued to offer advice and friendship, and additionally Fawzia Afzal-Khan, the late Meena Alexander, Tarek Al-Ghoussein, Awam Ampka, the late Michael Dash, Divya Dwivedi, Toral Gajarawala, Mélanie Heydari, Maya Kesrouany, Jean Khalfa, Ankhi Mukherjee, Ato Quayson, Arvind Rajagopal, Anupama Rao, Bruce Robbins, Mohamed-Salah Omri, Ella Shohat, Cliff Siskin, Bob Stam, Jini Watson. Once more, I warmly thank Badral Kaler for all that she has so generously given me over the years since this book was first published, and Maryam, Yasmine, and Isaac for still being themselves.

List of illustrations

1 New Jalozai refugee camp,
Peshawar, Pakistan,
November 2001: an Uzbek
family recently arrived **14**
© Jean-Marc Giboux.

2 New Jalozai refugee camp,
Peshawar, Pakistan,
November 2001: a young
Afghan boy flies a kite **15**
© Jean-Marc Giboux.

3 A Palestinian schoolgirl walks
in the ruins of a refugee camp
in Rafah in southern Gaza
Strip, 15 April 2001 **19**
Reuters / Damir Sagolj—stock.
adobe.com.

4 An early UNRWA school,
Jalazone refugee camp,
West Bank, 1951 **19**
© 1950 UNRWA Archive
Photographer Unknown.

5 Baghdad Peace review,
1918 **56**
Author's collection.

6 'Palestine Bantustan': map of
the West Bank after the Oslo
Agreement **72**

7 Mexico in 1824 **75**
Giggette / Wikimedia Commons
(CC BY-SA 3.0).

8 Cover of raï
compilation CD **89**
Courtesy of Manteca World Music.

9 'Arab woman' **93**
Author's collection.

10 Subcomandante Marcos
arriving in Mexico City, 10
March 2001 **98**
Reuters / Reuters
Photographer—stock.adobe.com.

11 'Muslim woman in Brooklyn'
by Chester Higgins Jr **101**
© Chester Higgins Jr. All rights
reserved.

12 Egyptian women volunteer for
popular resistance movements

against British
occupation **109**

Taken from Wassef &
Wassef: Daughters of the Nile,
American University in Cairo
Press, 2001.

13 Phoolan Devi, with her
gang, on her way to the
surrender ceremony at the
village of Bhind, India,
12 February 1983
(*Yagdish Yadar*) **116**

CPA Media Pte Ltd / Alamy
Stock Photo.

14 Chipko tree-huggers, northern
India, 1997 **134**

Photo by Bhawan Singh / The India
Today Group via Getty Images.

15 'Damn You Dam Makers':
local women protest against
the construction of the
Narmada Dam, Maheshwar,
India, 1999 **138**

© Ian Berry / Magnum Photos.

16 Frantz Fanon **146**

Everett Collection Inc / Alamy
Stock Photo.

The publisher and the author apologize for any errors or omissions in
the above list. If contacted they will be pleased to rectify these at the
earliest opportunity.

Introduction: montage

Have you ever been the only person of your own colour or ethnicity in a large group or gathering? It has been said that there are two kinds of white people: those who have never found themselves in a situation where the majority of people around them are not white, and those who have had the experience of being the only white person in the room. At that moment, for the first time perhaps, they discover what life is like for other people in their society who are not part of the majority, and, metaphorically, for much of the rest of the world outside the West: to be from a minority, to live as the person who is always in the margins, to be the person who never qualifies as the norm, the person who is not authorized to speak.

This is as true for peoples as for persons. Do you feel that your own people are somehow always positioned outside the mainstream, the centre of things? Have you ever felt that the moment you said the word 'I', that 'I' was someone else, not you? That somehow you were not the subject of your own sentence? Do you ever feel that when you speak, or try to speak, you have already in some sense been spoken for? Or that when you hear others speaking, that you are not included, that you are only ever going to be the object of their speech? Do you sense that those speaking would never think of trying to find out how things seem to you, how they look for you, from where you are? In short, that you live in a world of others, a world that exists *for* others?

How can we find a way to talk about this? That is the first question that the diverse writings now grouped under the term postcolonialism try to answer. The publication in 1978 of *Orientalism: Western Representations of the Orient* by the influential Palestinian-American critic Edward W. Said energized a range of different writers, academics, and activists to strategize as to how best to shift, to 'decolonize', the dominant ways in which the relations between Western and non-Western people, their cultures, and their worlds are viewed and valued. What does that mean? It means turning the world upside down, understanding and speaking of how differently things look when you live in Baghdad or Benin rather than Paris or Washington, and understanding why. It means realizing, as Said argued, that when Western people look at the non-Western world what they see is often more a mirror image of their own assumptions than the reality of what is there, or of how people outside the West actually feel and perceive themselves. If you are someone who does not identify yourself as Western, or as somehow not completely Western even though you live in a Western country, or someone who is part of a culture and yet feels excluded by its dominant voices, inside yet always outside, then postcolonialism offers you a way of seeing things differently, a language and a politics for how to reshape a world in which your interests come first, not last.

What was radical about Said's critique was not simply his demonstration that European accounts of the Orient repeatedly projected their own creation of a fantasmatic Eastern world, its exoticism founded on a whole set of racist assumptions, but that these attitudes permeated not just fictional or poetic writing but all written 'knowledge' about the East. Said's analyses ranged from fiction to political analysis, from the language of colonial administrators to scholarly academic studies, from anthropology to travel writing—and showed how everyone, though they may have been embedded in different genres or disciplines, subscribed to similar sets of assumptions about the East which they had learnt from earlier books. The result was that when a writer such as Flaubert went to the Middle East, he recognized only what he was expecting to see, rather as tourists today feel they have seen and know the real Paris only once they have seen the Eiffel Tower, or imagine they have experienced real native culture when they have seen an 'authentic' performance of a traditional dance which is now in fact only ever performed for tourists, the transient travelling colonials of our own times. In academic studies, orientalist scholars also articulated racist assumptions about the people whom they discussed. Said argued that the academic knowledge developed about the non-Western world served to facilitate colonial conquest and rule.

A range of influential ideas were developed in order to facilitate the critical study of these discursive aspects of colonialism. The first phase in which, following Edward Said, such attitudes were studied critically was known at the time as 'colonial discourse analysis'. This emphasized the implicit or explicit racism of European writing about the non-Western world, or the Eurocentrism of European knowledge, for example its attitudes towards history, in which the rest of the world only appears in the historical narrative when it becomes colonized by a Western power, such as in the European 'discovery' of America. Others, however, did not simply want to analyse the language of the colonial period by the Europeans of that era: they adopted the already-established term 'postcolonial', used to describe a former colony that had now become an independent state, in order to describe the perspective of those people who were once colonized but now independent; some writers used the term to evoke those who were taking positions critical of colonialism whether they were actually still colonized or not. 'Postcolonialism', therefore, which began to be used from the 1990s, is a term that represents perspectives critical of or resistant to colonialism or colonial attitudes.

The first place to look for such perspectives was in the writings of anti-colonial activists and philosophers from the colonial period, such as those of Frantz Fanon from Martinique or M.K. Gandhi from India. Other postcolonial academics emphasized what they called 'subaltern' perspectives, that is, the perspectives not of the political leaders but those of ordinary people, particularly women; others foregrounded the continuing cultural effects of colonialism, and the ways in which as a result of colonial invasions, all cultures have become increasingly mixed, or hybridized. These ideas will be discussed in more detail below. In the 21st century, particularly among those identifying with the non-white cultures of the Americas, emphasis moved away from the historical focus on colonialism and its era to the continuing need to combat residual social, cultural, and political attitudes or institutional practices that endure in the present, especially those displaying racist assumptions that go back to colonial perspectives. Anti-colonial thinkers had always insisted that decolonization had to begin not so much with the colonizers but with colonized peoples decolonizing themselves mentally from the ways in which they had been taught to see things from the perspective of the colonizers. The term 'decolonization' is now widely used as a metaphor for such cultural revisioning. Today, though formal colonialism has for the most part been defeated, we still need to extract ourselves from its living aftermaths.

Colonialism was a system that created rigid structures of profound inequality at many levels, justified ideologically by the doctrine of race. Postcolonialism resists such inhumanity: it assumes and claims the right of all people on this earth to the same material and cultural well-being, the same rights and the same access to impartial justice. The reality, though, is that the world today is a world of inequity, and much of the difference still falls across the broad division between the peoples of the West and those of the non-West. This division between the West and the rest was precipitated from the 16th century onwards by the expansion of the European empires through the use of state-organized violence, as a result of which by the early 20th century, nine-tenths of the entire land surface of the globe came to be controlled by European, or European-derived, powers. As the American political scientist Samuel P. Huntingdon has pointed out, Westerners now often forget this fact, but non-Westerners never do.

Throughout the period of colonial rule, colonized people contested this domination through many forms of active and passive resistance. While there were many acts of rebellion and resistance, large and small, for the most part it was only towards the end of the 19th century that such opposition developed into coherent political movements: for millions of the earth's inhabitants, much of the 20th century involved the long struggle and eventual triumph against colonial rule, often at enormous cost of life and resources. In Asia, in Africa, in the Caribbean, people fought against the politicians, administrators, and military forces of European powers that ruled the empires or the colonists who had settled in their world.

When national sovereignty was finally achieved, each state moved from being a colony to autonomous, postcolonial status. Independence! However, in many cases this represented only a beginning, a relatively minor move from direct to indirect rule, a shift from colonial rule and domination to a position not so much of independence as of being in-dependence. Despite decolonization, the major world powers did not change substantially during the course of the 20th century. Today, the same ex-imperial states often continue to dominate those countries that they formerly ruled as colonies. The contemporary histories of Afghanistan, Cuba, Iran, or Iraq make it clear that any country that has the nerve to resist its former imperial masters does so at its peril. All governments of these countries that have positioned themselves politically against Western control have suffered military interventions by the West against them.

Even so, the winning of independence from colonial rule remains an extraordinary, historic achievement. And if sovereignty remains limited, the balance of power has slowly been changing. For one thing, along with the shift from formal to informal empire, many Western countries require ever more additional labour power at home, which they fulfil through immigration. As a result of this, the clear division between the West and the rest in ethnic terms at least no longer operates absolutely. Cultures are changing: Barack Obama was elected President of the US, even if he was followed by Donald Trump. White Protestant America is being Hispanized as well as Africanized in a whole range of ways. From the beginning of the 20th century, black America operated as the dynamic motor of much Western culture, above all in music, that challenged the conservative culture of the heritage industry. More generally, the dominance of Western culture, which symbolized the division between Western and non-Western peoples, has been dissolving into a more inclusive system of tolerance and cultural respect for differences. Some of the limits of that respect will be explored in later sections of this book.

For now, what is important is that postcolonialism involves first of all the argument that the global South, the tricontinental countries, that is the nations of the three non-Western continents (Africa, Asia, Latin America, while not forgetting Oceania), for the most part remains in a situation of subordination to Europe and North America, typically in a position of economic inequality. Postcolonialism names a politics and philosophy of activism that contests that disparity, and so continues in a new way the anti-colonial struggles of the past. It asserts not just the right of African, Asian, and Latin American peoples to access resources and material well-being, but also recognizes the dynamic power of their cultures, cultures that are now intervening in and transforming the societies of the West.

No political or economic power structure is fixed. The world of the 21st century is no longer that of the decades of decolonization of the 1940s to the 1970s. That decolonization was precipitated by the Second World War and then facilitated by the ensuing Cold War between the capitalist and communist countries from 1945 to 1990. The collapse of the Soviet Union in 1991 was the spur for the spread of neo-liberal capitalist economics around the world, and this has changed both the economic and the political order. The global South now includes the richest as well as the poorest countries of the world: Brazil, China, and India make up three of the largest economies of the world, as well as 40 per cent of the world's population. This shift has been accompanied by greater inequality within Western countries: at the time of writing, the three richest American men collectively hold more wealth than the poorest 50 per cent of Americans (160 million people). The West is no more homogeneous than the South. However it not only retains much of its economic power, it also still controls the normative framework of global institutions and structures, from accounting to commerce to the Internet to legal systems to universities. The world as it is now organized internationally operates fundamentally according to European norms and values, starting with the nation-state.

The assumption that the Western way of doing things, or thinking about things, is always the best way is the legacy of the West's own economic military power and dominance, of which colonialism formed a part. As power shifts, so such assumptions get contested and transformed. The challenge to such expectations began during the resistance to colonialism in colonized countries; after decolonization, first in the colonized countries, and then later in the formerly colonizing cntries, attention shifted to what in 1986 the Kenyan writer Ngũgĩ wa Thiong'o called 'decolonizing the mind'. One of the most important aims of postcolonialism as a political and intellectual movement has been to decolonize its own cultures, and this has to be thought through at the local and personal levels. In what ways are you still colonized? How can you challenge practices that continue to enforce underlying colonial attitudes? We shall discuss this further in Chapter 1.

Postcolonial cultural analysis has been centrally concerned to develop theoretical structures that contest the previous dominant Western ways of seeing things. A simple analogy would be with feminism, which has involved a comparable kind of project: there was a time in Western countries when any book you might read, any speech you might hear, any film that you saw, was always told from the point of view of the man—because the male point of view was simply assumed to be the norm. The woman was there, but she always came second, typically as an object, never a subject. In what you would read, or the films you would see, the woman was always the one who was looked at. She was never the observing eye. For centuries it was assumed in many cultures that women were less intelligent than men and that they did not merit the same degree of education. They were not allowed a vote in the political system. By the same token, any kind of knowledge developed by women was regarded as non-serious, trivial, gossip, or alternatively as knowledge that had been discredited by science, such as superstition, witchcraft, or traditional practices of childbirth or healing. All these attitudes were part of a larger patriarchal system in which women were dominated, exploited, and physically abused by men. Slowly, but increasingly, from the end of the 18th century, feminists began to contest this situation. The more they contested it, the more it became increasingly obvious that these attitudes extended and filtered into the whole of the culture: into social relations, politics, law, medicine, the arts, popular and academic knowledges.

As a politics and a practice, feminism has not involved a single system of thought, inspired by a single founder, as had been the case with Marxism or psychoanalysis. It has rather been a collective work, developed by different women in different places in different directions: its projects have been directed at a whole range of phenomena of injustice, from domestic violence to law, from language to philosophy. Feminists have also had to contend with the fact that relations between women themselves are not equal and can in certain respects duplicate the same kinds of power hierarchies that exist between men and women. Nevertheless, broadly speaking feminism has been a collective movement in which women from many different walks of life have worked towards common goals, namely the emancipation and empowerment of women, the right to make decisions that affect their own lives, and the right to have equal access to education, to the law, to medicine, to the workplace, in the process changing those institutions themselves so that they no longer continue to represent only male interests and perspectives.

In a comparable way, 'postcolonial theory' involves a conceptual reorientation towards the perspectives of knowledges, as well as needs, developed outside the West. It seeks to drive forward ideas of a political practice morally committed to transforming the conditions of exploitation and poverty in which large sections of the world's population live out their daily lives. After Said's foundational volume, much early work in postcolonial theory was developed in India for an Indian context. Some of this theoretical work has gained a reputation for obscurity and for involving complex ideas that are difficult to understand. When faced with the authority of theory produced by academics, people often assume that their own difficulties in comprehension arise from a deficiency in themselves. This is unfortunate, since many of the ideas were never produced by academics in the first place and can be understood relatively easily once the actual situations that they describe are understood.

For this reason, this book seeks to introduce postcolonialism in a way not attempted before: rather than explaining it top down, that is, elaborating the theoretical ideas in abstract terms and then giving a few examples, it seeks to follow the larger politics of postcolonialism which are based in the experiences of ordinary people and affirm the worth of their cultures. Postcolonialism will be elaborated here not from a top-down perspective but from below: many of the sections that follow will start with a specific situation and then develop the ideas that emerge from its particular perspective, in other words from the ground up, which is where it should be, given that postcolonialism elaborates a politics of 'the subaltern', that is, of subordinated classes and peoples.

Postcolonial theory, so-called, is not in fact a theory in the scientific sense, that is, a coherently elaborated set of principles that can predict the outcome of a given set of phenomena. Nor does it form a structured methodology for the analysis of data, in the manner of the social sciences. It comprises instead a related set of perspectives, which are juxtaposed against one another, sometimes dialectically, that is, in creative opposition, and on occasion contradictorily. Different writers have put forward a range of overlapping but distinct arguments, involving issues that are often the preoccupation of other disciplines and activities, particularly to do with the position of women, of development, of ecology, of social justice, of socialism in its broadest sense. Much emphasis is placed on subjective lived experience. Postcolonial practice is oriented not simply towards analysis but also to intervention, inserting its alternative knowledges into the power structures of the West as well as the non-West. It seeks to change the way people think, the way they behave, to produce a more just and equitable relation between the different peoples of the world.

There is thus no single entity called 'postcolonial theory': postcolonialism, as a term, describes practices and ideas as various as those within feminism or socialism. The book therefore is not written as a series of chapters that develop an overall sequential thesis or argument as in the standard model of academic writing. Instead it uses the technique of montage to juxtapose issues and perspectives against one another, seeking to generate a creative set of relations between them: relationality is key. Postcolonial theory involves not static ideas or practices but creative interconnections: relations of harmony, relations of conflict, generative relations between different peoples and their cultures. It is the product of a changing world, a world that has been changed by struggle and which its practitioners seek to change further. Any discussions of theory in this book will be made in this context.

Fundamentally, postcolonialism is about changing your mind-set and your values. This is why postcolonial thinking disturbs the order of the world. It threatens privilege and power. It refuses to acknowledge the superiority of Western cultures, though without discrediting or rejecting them. Its radical agenda is to demand equality and well-being for all human beings who dwell on our planet, that there should no longer be any wretched of the earth.

You will now be migrating across that rough postcolonial terrain, experiencing its shocking contradictions and disjunctive juxtapositions. In the chapters that follow you will encounter its cities, the suburbs of its dispossessed, the poverty of its rural landscapes. These scenes will not add up: their relations are uneven, many of them are invisible, the lives and daily experiences of their inhabitants even more so. The chapters of this book present different 'scenes', snapshots taken in various locations around the world and juxtaposed against one another. This book therefore amounts to a kind of photograph album, but not one in which you are just gazing at the image, made static and unreal, turned into an object for your consumption divorced from the tremors of the real. These are stories from the other side of photographs that bear witness to the pain of actuality. Testimonies from the people who are looking at you as you read about them. The montage has been left as a rough cut that deliberately puts incompatible splintered elements side by side. A series of shorts that stage the contradictions of the history of the present, by catching its images fleetingly at a standstill. These fragmentary, arrested moments also trace a larger political journey of translation and transformation, from the disempowered to the empowered.

Chapter 1
Subaltern knowledges

You find yourself a refugee

You wake one morning from troubled dreams to discover that
your world has been transformed. Under cover of night, you have
been transported elsewhere. Before you open your eyes, you hear
the sound of the wind blowing across flat, empty land.

You find yourself walking with your family along the ungovernable
borderlands between Afghanistan and Pakistan. Towards
Peshawar, city of flowers, city of spies. A frontier town, the
traditional first stop for travellers from Kabul who have passed out
through the carved city gate of Torkham, down the long narrow
curves of grey rock of the Khyber Pass to the flat plain that lies
beyond, to the Grand Trunk Road that runs, stretches, streams all
the way to Kolkata.

In the Old City, among the many shops and stalls in the Khyber
Bazaar around the Darwash mosque, you find a narrow street
where the houses climb into the sky with their ornamented
balconies exploding out towards each other. This street is known
as the Qissa Khawani Bazaar, the street of storytellers. Over the
centuries, fabulous intricate tales have been elaborated here
between men relaxing over bubbling amber *shishas*, trying to
outdo the professional storytellers, or amongst those more quickly

sipping thick sweet, syrupy tea in glasses at the chai stalls. In old days this street furnished a romantic exotic destination for foreign travellers and tourists, but they no longer dare come to Peshawar; the stories that are being traded there now are not for you.

You are far to the west, beyond the colonial cantonment, beyond the huge suburbs of temporary housing of those who have arrived long since, out into the flats that lie before the mountains. The rest of your family, two of your children, are missing. You are carrying with you a bag of clothes, a mat, for prayer and sleep, a large plastic container for water, and some aluminium pots. Soldiers on the road stop you from walking further. The Jalozai refugee camp, the 'living cemetery' near Peshawar, has been closed, its inhabitants transferred to remote new sites at Kotkai, Old Bagzai, Basu, Shalman, and Ashgaro in the Khyber, Bajaur and Kurram agencies in the so-called Tribal Areas. Pashtuns who make it through from Afghanistan are shepherded towards Chaman, officially not a refugee camp but a waiting area or 'staging' camp just a few hundred metres from the border. Here, once your eye moves above tent level, the earth is flat and featureless until it hits the dusky distant shapes of the Himalayan foothills on the horizon.

Since this is not an official refugee camp, there is no one here to register you or mark your arrival. While your children sit exhausted and hungry on the bare, sandy brown earth, the skin on their blown bellies marked with the crimson stars of infection, you go in search of water and food, and with the hope of being issued with materials for housing—three sticks of wood and a large plastic sheet (Figure 1). This will be your tent, where you and your family will be living—that is, those who manage to survive the lack of food, the dehydration, the dysentery, the cholera. You may leave within months. Or, if you are unlucky—like the Somali refugees in Kenya, the Palestinian refugees in Gaza, Jordan, Lebanon, Syria, the West Bank, or the 'internally

1. New Jalozai refugee camp, Peshawar, Pakistan, November 2001: an Uzbek family that recently arrived in New Jalozai from northern Afghanistan is seen here in their new home.

displaced persons' in Sri Lanka or the South Africa of the 1970s—you may find that you are to be here for a decade, or for several. This may be the only home your children, and your grandchildren, will ever have.

Refugee, migrant, asylum seeker—whatever the term that translates you from a human being to a category—forced to leave your home you have become unsettled, uprooted, uncertain. You are mobile, mobilized, stumbling along your line of flight. But nothing flows. In moving, your life has come to a halt. Your existence has been fractured, your family fragmented. The lovely dull familiar stabilities of the ordinary, the everyday, and the local community that you have known have passed (Figure 2).

You have experienced the violent disruptions of capitalism as if compressed into a moment, the end of the comforts of the commonplace. You have become an emblem of everything that

2. New Jalozai refugee camp, Peshawar, Pakistan, November 2001: a young Afghan boy flies a kite.

people have been experiencing in cold modernity across different times for the last 200 years. You encounter a new world, a new culture to which you have to adapt while trying to preserve your own recognizable forms of identity. Putting the two together is an experience of pain. Perhaps one day you, or your children, will see it as their own, but not now. Life has become too fragile, too unpredictable. You can count on nothing. You have become an object in the eyes of the world. Who is interested in your experiences now, in what you think or feel? Politicians of the world's nation-states rush to legislate to prevent you from entering their countries. Asylum seeker: barred. You are the intruder. You are untimely, you are out of place. A refugee torn from your own land, carrying your body, beliefs, your language and your desires, your habits and your affections, across to the strange subliminal spaces of unrecognizable worlds. Everything that happens in this raw, painful experience of disruption, dislocation, and dis-remembering fuels the cruel but paradoxically creative crucible of the postcolonial.

15

Urban civilization has existed in Afghanistan for 5,000 years. In modern times, refugees have been fleeing the country since 1979 as a result of civil war and successive Russian and US invasions. Civil war and incursions by foreign powers were also the catalyst for the refugee crisis in Syria since 2011 with five million Syrians leaving the country, and six million displaced internally. What made this different in political terms was that as well as fleeing to refugee camps in nearby countries in the Middle East—Egypt (120,000), Jordan (1.4 million), Lebanon (1.5 million), Iraq (250,000), Israel (100), Kuwait (120,000), Turkey (3 million)—from August 2012 refugees also began to arrive in Europe by boat or on foot, creating what became known as the European migrant crisis. By 2015 arrivals amounted to over a million a year. Less than half of them were Syrians: the others included Afghanis, Iraqis, as well as migrants from many countries in Africa who often arrive by boat across the Mediterranean, usually via Libya. These people were moving for a variety of different reasons: civil war, drought, persecution, sheer poverty. While the response from Europeans and their politicians was initially humanitarian and sympathetic, as the flow continued and the refugees began to reach countries such as Hungary with no sea or land borders close to Africa or the Middle East, responses began to sour and precipitated protectionist populist nationalisms. Refugees and migrants began to be demonized, as with so-called 'illegals' in the United States. Since the first edition of this book in 2003, the number of refugees and 'internally displaced people' in the world today has tripled (it is now over sixty million).

Global migration is not simply a contemporary problem: historically, refugees and mass migration were initiated as a by-product of the formation of the nation-state as it attempted to regularize its population—the word 'refugee' was first applied to the Protestant Huguenots who were expelled by Louis XIV from France in the 17th century. Its meaning has always been double-edged: as V. S. Naipaul suggests in his own novel of migration, *The Enigma of Arrival* (1987), the word 'refuge' and 'refuse' (in both senses) can become uncannily interchangeable. For the next 200 years, millions of Europeans migrated in the hope of a better life from Europe to the European colonies. Around fifty-five million people moved to the United States alone in the hundred years from the 1840s to the 1940s. Within the United States itself, there were also forced migrations of indigenous peoples, the 'Great Migration' of six million African-Americans out of the rural South to the industrial North in the 20th century, people whose ancestors had themselves been forcibly migrated from Africa as slaves in previous centuries. In Europe, the end of both world wars and the refashioning of empires as nation-states produced the migration of millions of stateless people, as did the decolonization of British India in 1947. Measures enacted by the Nazis in Germany after 1933 forced hundreds of thousands of Jews, communists, and other 'undesirables' out of Germany; under the Haavara Agreement of 1933, 200,000 German Jews emigrated to British Mandate Palestine. The establishment of the state of Israel in Palestine in 1948 involved the forced expulsion of around 700,000 Palestinians from their homeland. The declarations and discourse of human rights have comprised one major international response to this situation. However, declaring human rights for refugees, migrants, and stateless people has in practice proved ineffective because human rights require the possession of citizenship of a state that will enforce them—the very thing that such 'placeless people' lack. For them, human rights are mere fictions that live in the hollow place between the aspirations of humanist morality and the reality of immigration laws of the nation-state.

Different kinds of knowledge

To lose everything and to be forced to move to another country as a refugee, your only property your own body and the knowledge that you carry within you, must be one of the most extreme human experiences of deprivation and dehumanization, the more so since one effect seems to be that you immediately begin to lose your humanity in the sight of others, reduced as the Italian philosopher Giorgio Agamben has put it, to 'bare life', an unrelenting minimal existence in which you are no longer the subject of rights but a supplicant who at best has become an object of compassion.

No one, though, can take away your own self, what you know, your knowledge of the world. Knowledge comes in two forms: experientially—the 'university of life' as Leopold Bloom puts it in James Joyce's *Ulysses* (1922)—and institutionally through formal education. The boundary lines between the two are more than fluid. The knowledge that you need literally to survive is the knowledge you learn informally, from your own family and environment. The knowledge you learn formally is someone else's knowledge, in which you are instructed. Who authorized it? Whose knowledge is it? Where does it come from? The knowledge that you learn in different schools will not be the same, and the frame of mind in which you learn will not be the same either: think of the differences for children between those who attend private schools in the West, such as Le Rosey in Switzerland whose 2019–20 tuition fees were $130,000 a year, and the learning experiences of the Palestinian girl in Figure 3, who walks to school through the ruins of the Rafah refugee camp where she lives, where the day before three Israeli tanks and two bulldozers had reduced the buildings to rubble.

The Rafah refugee camp in the south of Gaza was opened in 1949. Not a lot has changed in the seventy years since schools were first held in the open air at Khan Yunis refugee camp, Gaza Strip, or at the Jalazone refugee camp in the West Bank shown in Figure 4. If they are still alive, those boys standing on the bare stones in the open air are now old men, living in refugee camps that are themselves habitual targets for military strikes. How does it feel to have lived through such a life, invisible and forgotten?

3. A Palestinian schoolgirl walks in the ruins of a refugee camp in Rafah in southern Gaza Strip, 15 April 2001. This happened a day after Israeli forces attacked the camp in the second incursion in less than a week into an area that Israel had handed over to full Palestinian control under interim peace deals.

4. An early UNRWA school, Jalazone refugee camp, West Bank, 1951.

Thinking of these schools helps us to understand the perspectives from which postcolonial theory has been generated. Imagine what it is like to grow up in a close, deprived but warm and creative community, and then see its buildings literally bulldozed to the ground on the orders of the state. Here is Bloke Modisane's account of the destruction of Sophiatown, the vibrant centre of black cultural life in Johannesburg, by the South African apartheid government in 1958:

> Something in me died, a piece of me died, with the dying of Sophiatown....In the name of slum clearance they had brought the bulldozers and gored into her body, and for a brief moment, looking down Good Street, Sophiatown was like one of its own many victims; a man gored by the knives of Sophiatown, lying in the open gutters, a raisin in the smelling drains, dying of multiple stab wounds, gaping wells gushing forth blood; the look of shock and bewilderment, of horror and incredulity, on the face of the dying man.

Modisane doesn't allow us, though, to make the mistake of assuming that such experiences, such differences between the privileged and the wretched of the earth, only involve questions of suffering and deprivation. There are other kinds of riches, other kinds of loss. Other kinds of ways of thinking about the world. Human, rather than material.

Knowledge, politics, and power

See a picture of children who are assembling at a school, standing barefoot on stones, and you know you are in 'the third world'. This third world is the postcolonial world. The term 'third world' was originally invented during the Cold War on the model of the Third Estate (i.e. the bourgeoisie and the working class) from the time of the French Revolution in order to describe those countries which were not aligned to the two major political blocs, the capitalist West and the communist East. The third world was made up of what was left over: the new independent nations that had formerly made up the colonies of the imperial powers. At the Bandung Conference of 1955, twenty-nine recently independent African and Asian countries, including Egypt, Ghana, India, and Indonesia, initiated what became known as the Non-Aligned Movement. They saw themselves as an independent power bloc, with a new 'third world' perspective on political, economic, and cultural global priorities.

It was an event of enormous importance, symbolizing the common attempt of the people of colour in the world to throw off the yoke of the dominant capitalist and communist nations. Politically, they envisaged a third way, neither that of the West nor that of the Soviet bloc. However, that third way was slow to be defined and developed as an independent identity; in practice it was hard not to align informally with one of the two great powers. Gradually the term third world became associated with the economic and political problems that such countries encountered after independence, and consequently with poverty, famine, political instability. The German philosopher Hannah Arendt remarked that 'the third world is not a reality but an ideology'. In saying this, she put her finger on it, even if she meant her comment to be a criticism: the third world is a political idea and ideal. To give up on the term 'the third world' now is also to give up on the memory of a potent political history during which the greatest political actors, such as the Martiniquan psychiatrist, philosopher, and anti-colonial activist Frantz Fanon, one of the earliest to use the term, offered their ambitious and visionary plans for the future of the world of people of colour.

In opening up the possibility of a third way for subordinated peoples, the Bandung Conference marks the origin of postcolonialism as a self-conscious political philosophy. A more militant version of third-world politics, as a global alliance resisting the continuing imperialism of the West, came eleven years later at the great Tricontinental Conference held in Havana in 1966. For the first time, this event brought Latin America (including the Caribbean) together with Africa and Asia—the three continents of the South, hence the name 'tricontinental'. The conference established a magazine and newsletter (*Tricontinental Magazine* and *Bulletin*) which for the first time brought together the writings of many who would later be characterized as 'postcolonial' theorists and activists (Amilcar Cabral, Frantz Fanon, Che Guevara, Ho Chi Minh, Jean-Paul Sartre), elaborated not as a single political and theoretical position but as a transnational body of work with a common aim of popular political and cultural liberation, set out using innovative techniques of design in its artwork and famous posters that were as radical as its politics.

As terms, both 'tricontinental' and 'third world' retain their power because they suggest an alternative cultural dynamic, and, going beyond that, alternative 'epistemologies' or forms of knowledge. Most of the writing that has dominated what the world calls knowledge has been produced by people living in Western countries in the past three or more centuries, and it is this kind of knowledge that is elaborated within and sanctioned by the university, the official institutional knowledge corporation. There are many other kinds of knowledge that have their origins elsewhere. Historically this is even true for Western knowledge itself: much important early mathematical, medical, and scientific knowledge, for example, came from the Arab world, which is why today even Westerners write in Arabic every time they write down a number, and why algebra takes the form of an Arabic word (al-gebra). This transnational origin of mathematics and science has been largely forgotten, just as colonialism tried to erase the history of the peoples whom it ruled: as the Bissau-Guinean and Cape Verdean agricultural engineer, political theorist, and anti-colonial revolutionary Amilcar Cabral wrote in 1973 of African peoples:

> The colonialists usually say that it was they who brought us into
> history: today we show that this is not so. They made us leave

history, our history, to follow them, right at the back, to follow the progress of their history.

Postcolonial thought starts out from the possibilities prompted by such transcultural histories, which offer other kinds of knowledge and cultural perspectives to those which dominate the world. The self-conscious attempt to decolonize the mind and reappropriate repressed or devalued knowledges was an initiative of many early anti-colonial thinkers who challenged the hierarchy of knowledge in which non-Western cultures were recognized as the object of knowledge of outsiders such as Western anthropologists or orientalists, but were never regarded as a source of legitimate knowledge in themselves. Today, postcolonial thought starts from the premise that those in the West, both within and outside the academy, should take what the French philosopher Michel Foucault called 'historically subjugated knowledges' seriously and use them as a fulcrum from which to question their own assumptions. The terms 'postcolonial' and the more recent 'decolonial' signal the presence of these insurgent knowledges that come from the peripheries, from the indigenous, the marginalized, the dispossessed, and seek to transform the terms and values under which we all live. You can learn such knowledge anywhere if you want to. The only qualification you need to start is to stop looking at the world from above, and start to experience it from below, from those who live on the fringes, not at the centre.

We will now briefly consider some different perspectives that such reorientation brings with respect to histories, languages, and literatures.

Subalternity and the subaltern woman

In the 1980s a group of Indian historians, inspired by Mao Zedong's emphasis on the revolutionary role of the peasantry, started *Subaltern Studies*, a journal designed to consider the role of the peasantry in the recent history of India given that peasants had tended to be ignored by the then dominant groups of nationalist and Marxist historians. The editor, Ranajit Guha, explained in an opening editorial that he took the term 'subaltern' from the Italian Marxist Antonio Gramsci, who adapted it from its original military meaning of 'the ranks', that is, the mass of ordinary soldiers who served under the officers. Gramsci, who was himself particularly concerned with the political place of the peasantry in Italy, wanted a word less specific than the standard Marxist category of the 'proletariat' who perform a specific role in the process of industrial production, but which would still suggest the working people who are without power, living at the bottom of the social scale. Guha adapted Gramsci's term to his own definition of the condition of 'subalternity', which he defined as 'the general attribute of subordination in South Asian society whether this is expressed in terms of class, caste, age, gender and office or in any other way'.

The term was quickly adapted and extended to describe any marginalized or disempowered individual or group in contemporary society, particularly with respect to gender and ethnicity. Early interest focused on subaltern consciousness—that is, not analysing subaltern people or groups as a category from the outside, as would be the way of sociologists, but on how subaltern peoples themselves think, see, and speak the world. To retrieve their voices from the past requires a particular kind of archival work and retrieval, since typically formal archives preserve the records of the ruling class. It is possible to find scattered traces in the archive, for example law court records, but as the Indian critic Gayatri Spivak quickly pointed out, quite often, particularly in the case of women, especially working-class women or women of colour, they are just absent: we do not find their voice because they were never able to be in a position to speak. The Algerian/ Amazigh/French writer Assia Djebar, and the African-American writer Toni Morrison, have shown how one way to respond to this gap in the history of women is to reimagine it. Their novels, *Fantasia: An Algerian Cavalcade* (*L'Amour, La Fantasia,* literally

Love, Fantasia, 1985) and *Beloved* (1987) offer us powerful stories of Algerian women under French colonialism and African-American former women slaves in the United States told in their own words. In that context, history becomes rich and full of affect as the women from the past come back to life and tell their stories for the first time.

Languages

Different knowledges are not just produced by subordinated groups with their individual cultures and histories but are also articulated in their different languages. Of the 6,000–7,000 languages in the world today, 97 per cent of people speak only 4 per cent of them. Just 3 per cent of the world's population, for the most part indigenous peoples, speak the remaining 96 per cent of its languages. Each language embodies a particular mode of communicating, knowing, and knowledge of the world, while making up a part of the whole global language system. One of the ways in which colonial rule most alienated colonized people from themselves was through the devaluation of their languages. In almost every case, colonial rule established the colonizer's language as the official language, of administration, law, and education, while the local languages which had previously fulfilled these functions were degraded to the status of 'native' languages or dialects and ignored. In order to get anywhere, you had to learn the colonizer's language.

Today, it has all changed—or rather not. You have to learn the former colonizer's language. Most of today's dominant world languages are those of imperial conquerors—Arabic, Chinese, English, French, Spanish. As international communication becomes easier and easier, the thousands of 'minor' languages spoken in the world struggle to survive. With publishing more and more controlled by international corporations, writers often write in one of the dominant languages even if it is not their own first language in order to gain access to a global readership as a writer of 'world literature'. The official, authorized knowledge of the university, particularly in the sciences, is increasingly spoken and written in English. More and more universities around the world are teaching their courses in English. But does English actually make up a single language the world over? Probably no more than Chinese. Is a written language the same as the spoken language that bears the same name? There is in fact no intrinsic reason why we should speak and write in the same language. Modern English developed in the 15th and 16th centuries as a result of the championing of the vernacular spoken language rather than Latin in state and church institutions; paradoxically, today the majority of people who use English speak or write it as their second or third language. It has become the language of international communication, the global lingua franca functioning as Arabic, French, Latin, or Swahili have done in the past though they were all more limited geographically.

Until the 20th century, European concepts of language were theorized on the model of dead, written languages (Latin, Sanskrit)—forms that do not necessarily correspond to how people speak or how languages work in everyday practice. In situations where people use more than one language, especially where there is no standard national language, they are generally not separated out as discrete language systems. In many parts of the world, for example the Maghreb (North Africa), the Caucasus, or north-east India, languages flow into one another, modulated according to the particular ranges of those engaged in conversation, part of a larger plurilinguistic system in which the meanings of words can be sustained by the implicit presence of vocabulary in what some might call a different language.

Most states enforce one or more official languages, but the official language(s) may be very different from the languages that the population speaks. The situation is not simply one of so-called multilingualism, since it involves first a power hierarchy, and second the much more profound difference between a formalized language and ways of speaking that may never have been subject to the official intervention of being standardized into a particular form of writing and therefore a single 'language'.

This situation can be very flexible and productive, making Western concepts of translation redundant. On the other hand, where there is also a strong presence of a standard language, it can produce forms of language anxiety, because you feel caught between different languages. Fanon's angst—and irritation—came with white people's racist assumption that because he was black, French was not his own mother tongue and that his 'natural' language was Creole. Any compliment on his excellent French was for him the biggest insult. In fact, he only spoke French at home, but for those who mediate between standardized international and local languages, things can be more complicated.

The Zimbabwean novelist Tsitsi Dangarembga defined the multiple identities of the postcolonial situation with Fanon's phrase 'nervous condition', which for her was the result of her existence being strung out between the incompatible layers of different cultures and their languages. When a colonial or dominant culture is superimposed through education, it can produce a nervous condition of ambivalence, uncertainty, a blurring of cultural boundaries, inside and outside, a dislocating otherness within. In her novel *Nervous Conditions* (1988), Tambudzai, the narrator who dreams of an education, walks into the house of her relative who is a headmaster who has adopted white ways. She immediately finds that she does not know where to sit, does not know how to read the conventional signs of a room, does not know which language it would be appropriate to use—English or Shona? As she looks up at the powerful black male, her double consciousness is crossed by the additional hierarchy of genders which cuts across both, subjected to the painfulness of what Fanon recognizes as a hybridized split existence, of trying to live as two different, incompatible people at once.

The negotiation between different identities, between the layers of different value systems (especially in the case of women, for whom the options can seem to be mutually contradictory), for many ethnic minorities forms part of the daily experience of living in a white world, or for people of the South of living in a world system dominated by the languages and cultural values of the North.

This division is sometimes simplified into the difference between those who simply accept Westernization that comes with globalization and those who want to retain their own cultural identity or religion. But for most the opposition is less clear-cut. It is not unusual for people to want both or neither at the same time, and why not? The nervous condition of postcolonial desire finds itself haunted by an ungovernable ambivalence.

This doubled state of living between and within two or more languages can however also work productively. Writers such as the queer Chicana-American feminist Gloria Anzaldúa or the Moroccan Abdelkabir Khatibi have highlighted how thinking and writing in two or three languages allows them to stake out new unoccupied conceptual zones and to articulate what Anzaldúa characterizes as creative 'boundary-crossing visions'.

Literatures

Writing in multiple languages is very different from the way that much literature was conceived in Europe in the 19th century or later in the anti-colonial period, when novelists would often follow a Marxist-inspired aesthetic of socialist realism, and write narratives that would symbolically represent the formation of the new nation. Even so they often encountered a problem with respect to the question of language. Education in most colonies was conducted in the colonizer's language, with the result that in the 20th century those living in British, French, Portuguese colonies—or even postcolonies—were faced with a dilemma: should they write in their own mother tongue, typically the local language, or in the language which they had learnt to write in, English, French, or Portuguese, with their rich array of literary resources? 'The colonial bilinguist', wrote the French-Tunisian writer Albert Memmi in 1957, 'suffers a cultural catastrophe which is never completely overcome'.

During the nationalist period, many writers emphasized the political necessity of writing in the local language, a strategy often easier for poetry than for other genres. Some, such as Gandhi or Ngũgĩ, made a deliberate decision to give up writing in the colonial language and switch to their mother tongue; others, such as Chinua Achebe from Nigeria, or Mia Couto from Mozambique, or the Anglophone or Francophone Caribbean writers who had no 'mother tongue' other than Creole available such as Édouard Glissant, argued that it was possible to write in an English or French or Portuguese that registered the fact that colonial languages had, through colonialism, become global languages that were no longer the exclusive cultural property of one nation. Wherever they were spoken and written, they were infused by local vocabulary and other cultural features. This second option has now become a popular choice with some postcolonial writers, especially since globalization has offered the possibility of much wider circulation of their work. Others, particularly poets, remain stubbornly attached to their own 'minor' languages which offer different epistemologies, perspectives, understandings, emotional resonance.

Postcolonial literatures have typically followed two genres. The first has been characterized as 'the empire writes back': the result of the fact that older generations of colonial settlers or colonized people were brought up not on their own local literature but that of the colonial metropole. Many early texts by colonial writers as a result are concerned to put forward local perspectives against those of the colonizers—so Jean Rhys, who was brought up in Dominica, noticed how in Charlotte Brontë's *Jane Eyre* (1847), Jane's narrative, which Western feminists used to invoke as the paradigmatic account of female empowerment, is one in which her success is achieved through the elimination of a woman from the Caribbean, Bertha Mason. Rhys's extraordinary *Wide Sargasso Sea* (1966) retells that narrative from Bertha's perspective. Many Caribbean and South American writers, notably Aimé Césaire, as well as others such as Ngũgĩ, have taken and offered reversals of Shakespeare's *The Tempest*, focusing on its animalistic portrait of the enslaved, native Caliban. Much of the work of the South African writer J. M. Coetzee draws on comparable resources (e.g. his 1980s novels *Waiting for the Barbarians* and *Foe*). The Moroccan critic Abdelfattah Kilito has described modern North African literature as inevitably doubled, since whatever language authors may write in they always feel the presence of European literature over their shoulder. This interaction with the colonial culture is also marked in a different way by the fact that much 20th-century colonial or postcolonial literature was written in the metropole—novelists such as Sam Selvon or V. S. Naipaul from Trinidad, or Mulk Raj Anand from India, for example, began their writing careers in London. Postcolonial writing as a result has been much concerned with offering different representations of metropolitan cultures as places of migrancy, with a resulting rich cultural, ethnic, and linguistic diversity—a characteristic found in Salman Rushdie's or Zadie Smith's work.

On the other hand, one of the pleasures that people enjoy in fiction by writers from other countries are the experiences that it offers of insights into different cultures. What we can call the anthropological novel has become one of the dominant genres of postcolonial literatures (the Indian novelist Amitav Ghosh is in fact a trained social anthropologist): here the novelist gives us a detailed portrait of the workings of a different society typically antithetical to that of the West. Whereas travel writing used to offer a personal but always Western view of the exotic experiences of foreign lands, that function has now been taken over by the non-Western novelist who performs the function of the anthropologist's 'native informant', so that today instead of reading travel writing Westerners read novels by writers from far-off countries. The best-selling African novel of all time, Chinua Achebe's *Things Fall Apart* (1958), is both a riposte to the demeaning representation of Africans in Joseph Conrad's *Heart of Darkness* (1899) and a patient anthropological account of the ordered seasonal life of a West African village. The first to practise this genre were European colonials such as Leonard Woolf, whose *The Village in a Jungle* (1913) does something similar for rural life in Ceylon (now Sri Lanka).

While much postcolonial writing shares these characteristics, and articulates in an evocative and experiential way many of the issues around migration, race, gender, history, and the decolonial that form the subject of this book, it has also redefined the scope of the literary itself, starting with the dissolution of the relation between literature and national languages. Although postcolonial criticism has been largely written in English or French, postcolonial literatures exist in many languages, small as well as the large or dominant. Creating much of the momentum that in the 21st century has broken down the idea of national literatures in favour of world literatures, the best contemporary postcolonial writing has come to challenge ideas of postcoloniality itself. It can be in this way too that literature always takes us to another place.

Chapter 2
Colonialisms, decolonization, decoloniality

How did this situation of 'postcoloniality' in which our world finds itself happen in the first place? For centuries, the peoples of Europe, particularly the Venetians, had traded with those of India and China, precious goods travelling overland along the Silk Road which ran from East to West or by sea on the spice trade routes of Asia. What became a Venetian monopoly encouraged the Portuguese and Spanish to find a sea route to India and China, either around the African coast, as in the case of Vasco da Gama, or by sailing due west, as in the case of Christopher Columbus, who happened upon the Americas, previously unknown to Europeans, instead. These trading voyages were to have the most profound unintended consequences: four centuries later, Europeans had colonized or semi-colonized four-fifths of the territory of the globe, causing millions of deaths by violence or disease in the process.

This colonization took two major forms: the first was where the colonizers gradually took over an area of land whose sovereignty was not established in a European way, or occupied a foreign state, and then administered and taxed it, but maintained little more than occupying troops, administrators, merchants, and missionaries. India would be an example of this kind of 'exploitation' colony, French Indo-China or Dutch Indonesia others. In these cases, colonial rule was increasingly contested—sometimes by political agitation, sometimes by military resistance—and in the decades after the Second World War many such countries gained independence. The postcolonial era involved each country not only establishing its own sovereignty but also decolonizing its institutions and culture where it wished to, or could do so, for example economically or in the areas of language and education.

The second form of colonization was very different because in addition to everything in the first, it involved an additional factor whose effect was much more profound: settlement by Europeans who arrived with the intention of adopting the colony as their permanent home. With a few exceptions, they and their descendants would never leave. While this was the earliest form of colonization—starting with the Spanish and Portuguese in the Americas in the 16th century, the continuing effects of such 'settler colonialism' remain painfully acute right up to the present day—not for the settlers, but for the indigenous peoples amongst whom they settled. In almost every instance the settlers, arriving armed with superior technology and imperial logistical support, were able to subdue, slaughter, or enslave the local inhabitants. In many islands of the Caribbean the indigenous population was wiped out; in Spanish America, it is estimated that eight million were killed or died of disease. (The term 'Latin America' has a problematic history: originally conceptualized by the French to give plausibility to their own imperial interventions in South America—they invaded Mexico in 1836–7, and briefly set up their own puppet monarchy there from 1861 to 1867—it was also developed by the Chilean philosopher-politician Francisco Bilbao and other members of the Creole elite to define themselves against invading Anglo-Saxon America to the north. For this reason, some prefer 'South America'; however what then gets lost is that Spanish America originally extended, and in some respects still extends, all the way north up to Oregon and westwards up to Louisiana).

Much early writing in postcolonial studies focused on analysing the effects of the first kind of colonialism, offering an alternative view of imperial history from the perspective of the colonized. This was articulated with earlier accounts from the 1950s, such as those by Césaire and Fanon (both from Martinique) or Albert Memmi (from Tunisia), of the psychology of colonization, that is, how living under colonial rule affects the subjectivity and consciousness of colonized people as individuals. As we have seen, anti-colonial activists, such as Fanon and Gandhi, argued that for colonized peoples decolonization began with decolonizing yourself: alongside with seeking the expulsion of the colonizer, it was important to undo all the ways that colonization had affected people's modes of seeing themselves and their own cultural assumptions and values. Intellectual decolonization had to accompany any attempts at political decolonization. Many of the major academic figures who emerged in the postcolonial field in the 1980s, such as Edward Said, or Homi K. Bhabha, Partha Chatterjee, Ranajit Guha, or Gayatri Spivak, were intellectuals who had been born in former British colonies; their writing articulated their experiences of living in a colonized society, together with their experiences as immigrants coming to study and then teach in universities in the UK or USA. In both cases, their analyses formed part of the process of decolonizing themselves and their academic disciplines at the same time. The key factor connecting the colonial past with the postcolonial present was the legacy of the production of racial ideology as justification for colonialism and slavery. The problem was not just the inequities of the past but the continuing effects of stereotyped racialized attitudes in the present.

Since its emergence in the 1980s, postcolonial studies has impacted on almost every discipline in the humanities and social sciences. In conjunction with related projects such as critical race studies, the kind of knowledge taught by universities and schools has been re-examined in almost every sphere, often with the result that Eurocentric perspectives, along with the lack of representation of people of colour, of women, of lesbian bisexual gay transgender queer plus (LBGTQ+) people, have become starkly apparent, whether in anthropology, history, law, literature, philosophy, political thought, or sociology. The decolonization of the university goes to the heart of many of its disciplines. In 2019 even Anglo-Saxon scholars woke up to the fact that their discipline was developed in the context of a political-racial project.

In the 21st century, as the memories of decolonization have receded into the past, many postcolonial scholars have moved on to focus on the more enduring second kind of colonization—that of settler societies, particularly in the Americas, Australasia, Ireland, the Middle East, and South Africa. While some settler colonies, such as those in Algeria, Kenya, or Zimbabwe, were decolonized and the indigenous people able to take back control, in the majority the settlers themselves gained independence from the colonial power and the indigenous people were left to their own fates as subjugated minorities or even majorities. This has led to comparative analysis of settler colonialism and the related but often distinct problems that it has produced, which has now become a significant field in its own right. And from the oldest arena of settler colonialism of all, South America, a specific, local form of critical thinking has been developed by a number of academics and activists, such as Walter Mignolo, Catherine Walsh, and Nelson Maldonado-Torres, known as 'the decolonial option' or 'decoloniality'.

Decoloniality

The concept of decoloniality has been the most important related formation to emerge alongside postcolonial studies in the 21st century; depending on the context it is sometimes distinguished from it but clearly also overlaps it in many ways. Decolonial thinking defines itself against the norms of postcolonial thinking in one fundamental aspect. While postcolonial studies followed the anti-colonial movements in contesting colonialism and imperialism utilizing primarily Marxist concepts that were designed to be universally applicable, decolonial thinkers and activists stress the fact that they are discussing the discrete situation of Latin America, even there emphasizing local histories of multiple formations. Postcolonial theory, for example in the work of Edward Said, has tended to place primary emphasis on the history of 19th-century imperialism and subsequent decolonization, quickly passing over the earlier centuries that witnessed the invasion and colonization of the Americas, almost all of which had become independent by the early 19th century, though, with the exception of Haiti, always under the control of the settler or Creole upper classes. Most of the Americas were independent before most of Africa had been colonized.

In the context of the radically disparate time schemes of colonization across five centuries, Mignolo emphasizes what he calls 'the colonial difference', by which he means that every colonized country has its own specific history of colonization, often operating in different temporalities that create particular conditions that cannot be simply generalized from one to another. In a similar way to decoloniality, we could say that contemporary related intellectual projects such as Afropessimism, caste and postcolonial studies have all developed according to different temporalities of their own.

Though it is argued that it is not a 'theory', decolonial thinking does, however, start with the general theoretical premise that colonialism and modernity were, globally, the two sides of the same coin. While most commentators trace the beginning of modernity, and what economists call the 'great [economic] divergence' between Europe and the rest of the world to the 18th century, Mignolo and others argue that the invasion of America (starting with Columbus' expedition in 1492) itself precipitated the beginnings of the modern era, particularly economically as the result of the transfer of vast amounts of gold and silver from America to Spain. This allows them to put the two together as a part of the same process. The argument that follows is that despite formal decolonization, what Mignolo calls 'the colonial matrix' still continues everywhere today. What he means here is that colonialism and imperial rule enabled Europe to establish ideological as well as physical control, dominance, or hegemony: this was not just capitalism as a system, the political organization of nation-states, and rationality as the basis for knowledge and thought, but also their embodiment in individual institutional disciplines and practices with which we all live every day. Even where some forms of Western knowledge have now been discredited, such as ideas about racial hierarchy, in practice the effects of this still live on, as every person of colour knows.

Colonization not only involved the extermination or subjugation of indigenous peoples but also of their local knowledges. As we have seen, Western rationalism and its epistemology discounts and devalues other kinds of knowledge, particularly those of people of colour and the global South. Even after decolonization many formerly colonized peoples, especially their leaders and the elite classes, continued to have Western mind-sets. In his earlier work, Mignolo emphasizes what he calls 'border thinking', a kind of hybrid thinking which is a version of Du Bois' double consciousness which Mignolo points to in the work of Anzaldúa, Néstor García Canclini, Fanon, Glissant, and Khatibi. Border thinking allows a critical facility from a quasi-outside which Mignolo claims enables the development of critical thinking of a different kind from the West's own radical internal critical tradition of Bartolomé de Las Casas, Jeremy Bentham, Karl Marx, and more recent thinkers such as the German philosophers Theodor Adorno and Max Horkheimer, who offered a critical account of Enlightenment thought in *Dialectics of the Enlightenment* (1944/7), or Michel Foucault, who critiqued the basis of the Enlightenment's concept of Reason in *Madness and Civilization* (1961).

In more recent work, Mignolo has emphasized the particular Latin American tradition of decolonial thought, including Christian liberation theology, dependency theory, Marxist world-systems theory, the Latin American Subaltern Studies historians, as well as South American anti-colonial activists and theorists, especially those who emphasized the epistemologies and knowledges of the indigenous peoples of South America, who, he argues, think 'otherwise', such as the Peruvian Marxist José Carlos Mariátegui or the Cuban anthropologist Fernando Ortiz. The most famous Latin American revolutionary, Che Guevara, however, is notable by his absence, presumably because he was a radical revolutionary advocating social change towards a communist society, wholly European in its conception, as were Caribbean radicals such as Césaire, C. L. R. James, Fanon, and Walter Rodney. With the exception of Fanon and Subcomandante Marcos, the radical revolutionary internationalist tradition of the Americas is of less significance in decolonial thought than the work of Argentinian/Mexican liberation philosophers such as Enrique Dussel, Rodolfo Kusch, and others.

More broadly the terms 'decoloniality' and 'decolonizing' have come to signify the attempt to resituate knowledge and everyday practice outside the dominant power structures of Western/ European/North American thought, with particular reference to people of colour who have been marginalized by that configuration, but also including peoples of marginal sexualities and ethnicities. Interest has moved away from articulating the inequities of colonial history or detecting signs of indigenous resistance in the past, to decolonizing the present. This shift from past to present forms part of the general contemporary waning of interest in history in favour of foregrounding the perspectives of today (simply put, the postmodern or 'transmodern' outlook that has come to dominate our own era). The need for decolonization today is precisely because we are postcolonial. It is not just the cultures of postcolonial countries that need to be decolonized, but even more so the cultures of the once-colonizing countries too, in particular, those countries of the Americas and Australasia whose settler populations became independent one or even two centuries ago. If the first phase of postcolonial studies was associated particularly with rewriting the histories of the Middle East and South Asia; in the second, attention has shifted to South America and its relation to its own colonial history and to the United States in the north.

In his *Discourse on Colonialism* (1950), Aimé Césaire attacked the European colonial tendency to destroy non-European cultures and then put their remnants in European museums. In the wake of such polemical critiques, decoloniality has developed into a practice which seeks to re-evaluate the past in all countries, colonizing and colonized, with particular attention not just to history as it is written, but also to the surviving material remains of that history, in institutions such as museums and universities, such as Belgium's vast Africa Museum, bursting with booty from the Belgian Congo. The 'Rhodes Must Fall' movement, which began in South Africa, spread to England, and then correlated with the Black Lives Matter movement in the US, highlighted some universities', churches', corporations', and other institutions' past profitable relation to colonialism and slavery.

And from there the term decolonize has expanded to ever more metaphorical forms of colonization, starting with current practices in race, gender relations, and moving on to almost every aspect of life and lifestyle—instagram post hashtags in the first group include #decolonizeeducation #decolonizehistory #decolonizethisplace #decolonizeyourmind #decolonizefeminism #decolonizeyoursyllabus #decolonizeyourbookshelf #decoloniseyourlife #decolonizemyself; and then expand to #decolonizeyourmedicine #decolonizing_mental_health #decolonizebirth #decolonizeyoga; and from there to #decolonizelove #decolonizeyourdiet #decoloniseyourwardrobe....Whatever the topic, as with environmentalism all these movements are designed to make people think critically not only about the history and power structures of their own cultures, but about their own daily lives within them: decolonize your everyday practices and those that you encounter around you. The scope of decolonial thinking has thus become extremely broad: it can be focused on almost any contemporary cultural, institutional, social, or political practice wherever you may live, but the important fact remains that it has been particularly meaningful for indigenous peoples and subjugated minorities who live in states that are historically white settler colonies where indigenous land rights, histories, languages, and cultures have been erased.

Chapter 3
Slavery, race, caste

Slavery, race, and racism

The most sustained form of early colonial violence involved the enslavement of millions of non-Europeans. Notwithstanding the success of the anti-slavery movement in the 19th century, the history of slavery, to invoke Karl Marx's phrase from *The Eighteenth Brumaire*, continues to weigh 'like a nightmare on the brains of the living'. The core of postcolonialism and decoloniality as contemporary practices involves the attempt to arrest, reconfigure, and transfigure the collective memory of slavery and the ideology of race which sustained it—as well as transforming the continuing social inequities which represent its direct legacy. That that memory remains so strong is hardly surprising in the context of generational memory: there are still people alive who remember Matilda McCrear, the last surviving former slave in the US, taken as a child from Africa, who died in 1940.

Slavery was not simply an oppressive system: it was given moral, ethical, and even philosophical justification by a broader ideology of race, which continued and indeed even strengthened after slavery was abolished. As imperialism expanded, theories of race that had been originally developed as a defence of slavery were elaborated into a justification of colonial rule of allegedly 'backward' peoples. Developed and sustained by academic anthropologists, medical scientists, natural and metaphysical philosophers, and philologists, racial theories portrayed the peoples of the colonized world as determined by their bodies which made them inferior, childlike, or 'feminine' in stereotyped ways, incapable of looking after themselves (despite having done so perfectly well for millennia) and requiring the paternal rule of the West for their own best interests (today many are still deemed to require 'development'). Race was the brazen ideology of empire from which we are all still struggling to free ourselves today, long after those empires have passed away. All races were put in a hierarchy of intelligence, with Europeans at the top and Aboriginal Australians at the bottom. White culture was regarded as, and indeed remains, the basis for ideas of legitimate government, law, economics, science, language, music, art, literature—in a word, 'civilization'.

While Marxism had provided a critique of the economic basis of colonialism, the intervention of postcolonial theorists was to point out that Marxism had ignored the impact of the ideas of racial difference that had provided the justification for domination during the period of colonial rule. The Marxist analysis was not rejected, it was simply critiqued as being too limited in its scope. It made no sense to ignore colonialism's ideological basis. One of the first to make this argument was the African-American Cedric J. Robinson in *Black Marxism: The Making of the Black Radical Tradition* (1983) where he developed the concept of 'racial capitalism'. Since slavery and colonialism were driven by the economic engine of capitalism, the idea of white racial superiority developed to justify slavery and the violence of imperial conquest and rule, reaching its apex in the 'scientific' racialism of the imperial era of the late 19th century, provided the justification for the capitalist exploitation of the non-Western world. Even though the majority of colonies have been decolonized, racial ideology survives in the widespread prevalence of racism today—that is what directly connects the colonial past to the postcolonial present. Postcolonialism will only be 'over' when racism, in all its many dimensions, has disappeared as a form of human relations. Whether and how this moment can be envisaged as a reality or as a utopian possibility forms the basis of connections to related fields with comparable concerns such as Afropessimism and critical race studies.

Slavery remains one of the most powerful reverberations of colonial rule. Today it affects not so much the African countries from which slaves were bought as those countries to which they were taken, primarily the Americas (Brazil, the Caribbean, the United States). As Paul Gilroy has argued, the system of slavery was not an isolated practice but formed part of a wider commercial activity involving the three continents of the Atlantic which he characterizes as the 'Black Atlantic'—Lisa Lowe adds Asia to what she calls the 'intimacies of four continents'. The slaves in Brazil, the Caribbean, and the southern states of the US were part of an international network of commodity trading and consumption that formed part of the early expansion of international capitalism. The plantations were the first factories.

There have now been many books on the history of race and racial ideology, or sociological books on race as a 'problem' in society as if it was the people of colour who were to blame. Until the 1950s, however, there were very few books written by people of colour describing and analysing the experience of how it felt to live in a racist society, and how best to struggle against this experience as a person. One of the earliest was Frantz Fanon.

Fanon had grown up in colonial Martinique, but it was only when he arrived in mainland France in 1946 that he found that he had unwittingly become a bizarre kind of spectacle because of the colour of his skin. He recounts that when he walked down the street, people called out: 'Look! A negro!' In *Black Skin, White Masks* (1952), Fanon comments:

> I came into the world imbued with the will to find a meaning in
> things, my spirit filled with the desire to attain to the source of the

world, and then I found that I was an object in the midst of other objects.

Fanon's first experience of racism brought the pain of, as he puts it, being 'sealed into that crushing objecthood', of being transformed from a 'me' to 'him', from a subject into an object. Later he realized that the problem went even deeper, that being turned into an object, the target of a pointing finger and a deriding gaze, was only the exterior part. What he understood was that in such situations people often come to internalize this external view of themselves, to see themselves as different, 'other', lesser. Growing up was about becoming two selves—yourself and that other invisible or hypervisible person into which you are translated when in a white world (in 1952, the very same year as Fanon's text, the African-American Ralph Ellison also wrote about this strange paradox of invisibility/over-visibility in his novel *Invisible Man*). In such a situation, you start to develop what the African-American philosopher W. E. B. Du Bois called a 'double consciousness'—conscious of yourself and of some other being:

> It is a peculiar sensation, this double-consciousness, this sense of always looking at one's self through the eyes of others, of measuring one's soul by the tape of a world that looks on in amused contempt and pity. One ever feels his two-ness,—an American, a Negro; two souls, two thoughts, two unreconciled strivings; two warring ideals in one dark body, whose dogged strength alone keeps it from being torn asunder.
>
> The history of the American Negro is the history of this strife—this longing to attain self-conscious manhood, to merge his double self into a better and truer self. In this merging he wishes neither of the older selves to be lost. He does not wish to Africanize America, for America has too much to teach the world and Africa. He wouldn't bleach his Negro blood in a flood of white Americanism, for he knows that Negro blood has a message for the world. He simply wishes to make it possible for a man to be both a Negro and an

American without being cursed and spit upon by his fellows,
without having the doors of opportunity closed roughly in his face.

For Fanon and Du Bois challenging racism has to begin with your
own consciousness and sense of self-worth. How though to climb
out of the abyss of the self into which you have been thrown? To
be a full person rather than split in two?

One of the ways would be to revalue your own culture and
language against those of the colonizer or dominant power—the
idea of *négritude* was developed by black French colonized
intellectuals in the 1930s to do exactly that—at which point you
can start to decolonize yourself. This has also been the practice of
others who find themselves in this racialized situation, such as the
Dalits in India.

Caste

Race and racial theory were invented as the ideological
justification for European colonialism and imperialism: its
contestation will always be central to any postcolonial politics.
Racism as such, however, is not exclusive to Western societies.
'Some years ago we were astonished to see for ourselves that the
North Africans despised black men', Fanon wrote of his
experiences in Morocco and Algeria during the Second World
War. Racial hierarchies operate in many societies around the
world, with fairness regarded as synonymous with beauty.

The prevalence of caste in South Asia shows how racist practices
extend further than slavery or European colonialism. Caste or
jaat, a form of segregation between social groups based on an idea
of religious duty, located on a hierarchy descending from the 'pure'
to the 'polluted', goes back thousands of years and remains deeply
entrenched in postcolonial Indian society. The caste system is
hereditary, defined at birth and fixed in your name; it indicates
degrees of purity, social status, and the kind of work which you

and your family were supposed to follow. Caste still determines forms of social organization from eating to marriage to where you are allowed to live.

The practice of caste is centred on the idea of proximity and touch: although a marker of respect, the distinctive Hindu 'namaste' greeting of holding your own hands together also conveniently avoids you having to touch the other person. Beneath the hierarchy of the four main castes (themselves divided into thousands of sub-castes), a further group, defined as those without caste, *achhoots* or outcastes, have been considered absolutely untouchable because they are thought to pollute anyone or anything with which they come into contact. About 16 per cent of the Indian population is made up of 'untouchables' or Dalits, as the more politicized call themselves (Dalit means 'the oppressed' or 'the broken'). Subjugated and exploited, they do the most menial jobs—the educated will work as clerks in a bank, others will be cleaning toilets, working with leather, or repairing roads—and live segregated from the rest of the population, in villages on the downhill side of the drainage ditch, in cities in *chawls* or low-income housing. Dalits have comparatively little access to education, or health care, and are forced to suffer daily the indignities of being considered unclean and polluting by the rest of the population (examples of discrimination include having to remove their shoes when they walk through the parts of the village where the higher castes live; not being allowed to sit on buses, to collect water from common wells, or enter Hindu temples). At the same time, the upper castes exploit them economically, materially, and sexually, and subject them to constant mental and physical abuse. Women from lower castes were traditionally forbidden to cover their breasts with a blouse, so as to ensure their constant availability for predatory upper-caste men. Even today, robbery of, attacks on, or rapes of Dalits are rarely taken seriously as crimes by the police, who generally disregard them and decline to take action against the perpetrators. The untouchable status of the Dalits is an intrinsic part of Hinduism and its ideology of purity.

Throughout the 20th century, there were many Dalit political movements contesting the degradation into which Dalits were born. The best known was led by the remarkable B. R. Ambedkar, who successfully negotiated for positive discrimination for Dalits in certain areas of Indian institutional practices, and drafted the Indian constitution in which these provisions were embodied. Ambedkar challenged the Hindu idea that the social order which determined caste was sacred and fixed. His 1936 essay 'Annihilation of Caste' (a speech he was asked not to deliver) provocatively argued that 'Hindus must consider whether they must not cease to worship the past as supplying its ideals'. 'In a changing society', he continued, 'there must be a constant revolution of old values'. Ambedkar's work, which constituted a profound and radical challenge to the vested interests of the Indian upper classes, has since provided the fundamental basis for social reform in India. It has also prompted scrutiny of the privilege of Brahmins and the upper castes, just as in the West whiteness with all its advantages has become the subject of interrogation.

The 21st century has witnessed a powerful national and international campaign for Dalit human rights. In practice, however, the situation has remained relatively unchanged. After the Gujarat earthquake of 2000, there were widespread reports that Dalits were being discriminated against in the distribution of relief. Even emergency earthquake aid was organized so as to correlate with the caste system. As a result of their degraded place in but out of Hinduism, some Dalits have converted to Christianity and Islam. Others, including Ambedkar and the Bandit Queen Phoolan Devi (who will be discussed below), converted to Buddhism. The drawback is that, in doing so, such converts lose the constitutional rights specifically allocated to Dalits that Ambedkar had won for them.

Unlike some minority groups elsewhere, Dalits embrace modernity in its international form, identified with rationality and

Western science, precisely because it is free of the values of Indian caste culture. Against the nationalist emphasis on Hindi and local Indian languages, they also advocate the use of English because as a language it is not permeated with caste markers. Even British colonialism gets praised because the British treated Dalits as human beings. Dalit politics thus runs counter not only to some Indian postcolonial arguments, but distinguishes itself from the 'decolonial' emphasis on indigeneity in some cultural politics of the Global South. The injustice of the indigenous Hindu social system that gives discrimination religious sanction is exactly what Dalits want to get away from.

India is not the only country to operate a caste system: in different forms it can be found in Bangladesh, Nepal, Pakistan, and Sri Lanka, as well as in China, Japan, and Korea, even in some parts of Africa. If caste means any discriminatory stratification based on family origin and inherited characteristics such as skin colour, it bears many similarities to the discrimination suffered by African-Americans in the United States, as W. E. B. Du Bois argued. One difference between them is that the sanctioned social prejudices of caste derive from the teachings of Hindu religion and its belief system, which makes any possibility of altering its embodiment in the social system more difficult.

A postcolonial politics is equally opposed to discrimination by caste or race, wherever or however it may be practised. It seeks to turn difference from the basis of oppression into one of positive, intercultural social diversity.

Chapter 4
History and power, from below and above

Notwithstanding the contemporary use of the word 'decolonize', decolonization has not, of course, lost its original literal meaning where it holds out the promise of future sovereignty for still-colonized lands—just as colonialism and imperialism are still often invoked in relation to the continuing interference by former colonial powers in the internal affairs of an independent decolonized state.

Countries that achieved sovereignty in the independence struggles often still find that they are the object of interventions by the Western countries that had once ruled them. Has the Middle East, for example, ever really been free of Western interference since Napoleon invaded Egypt in 1798 or the remnants of the Ottoman Empire were divided up between Britain and France at the end of the First World War?

Bombing Iraq—since 1920

I was standing on the balcony looking out over the skyline of yellow houses towards the dark limestone mountains of the north, which rose steeply into the evening sky. I could still make out the vast flag of Cyprus's Turkish Republic hanging across the mountainside, an enormous mosaic of bright painted stones laid out to make a crescent and star between two horizontal stripes, all red against a white background. Wherever you are in Nicosia, whenever you look north, you see that flag, floating defiantly across the skyline, with its uncompromising message written beside it: 'Ne mutlu turkum diyene'—'How happy to be a Turk'. It is over twenty-five years since the island was partitioned. The barbed wire on the United Nations line that divides the two sides is rusty, many of the command and lookout posts seem to have been long deserted. Yet virtually nothing moves across it; the two sides stare at each other still across walls, wire, and invisible mines of the divide, remembering their abandoned homes, the people in their families still missing, the nights when whole villages were massacred. One more lingering colonial effect that, coming after a hard-won independence struggle, could be blamed on the people themselves.

I watched the lingering light fading on the hills, listening to the *adhān al-maghrib*, the evening call to prayer, from the other side of the city. In the background, I could hear the sound of the Reuters emails coming in on the PC inside, as everyone all over the region filed in their evening reports. I looked back at the desk and saw there was a message from Khaled, who had recently been posted to Baghdad. I double-clicked the cursor on his name and his message came up.

From: Khaled   Sent: Wed 22/01/2003 23:08

To: Shayan

Cc:

Subject: Re. Report

Assalam alaikum. I managed to meet up at last tonight with that man I told you about. It was hard to get in touch, with everything that was going on at the office, and at his office too, where they're busy trying to move the treasures of the collection to somewhere safer—the National Museum is right by the main telephone exchange and the Foreign Ministry. Anyway, eventually we arranged to meet up at Al-Haj-Muhammad's, at the corner of Mustansír St. The conversation took an unexpected turn. Don't send the attached to the news desk—can you file it to features please? Also, ask Nick if he can get it syndicated. Thanks. K.

'The right to bomb': Baghdad, 21 January 2003

As I walked in, I saw him from the other side of the room, staring abstractedly at the diamond-patterned tiles on the floor, his hands wrapped together at the end of his thin arms. I sat down and he ordered coffee for us both. We spoke warmly of old mutual friends, of his years in Paris and in London. Sadiq is a Senior Deputy to the Director General of antiquities in Baghdad, specializing in Mesopotamian books of the Seljuk era. Some years ago, he published an impressive scholarly account of Dioscorides' *De Materia Medica* (1224 CE) and is now well-known as an authority on medical treatises of that era. He spent over a year in Paris studying the *Kitab ad-Diryak* (*The Book of Antidotes*, 1199 CE) at the Bibliothèque Nationale, analysing the exquisite illustrations in the book of the cultivation of plants for their medicinal properties. I wanted to know more about the role of plants and herbs in medicine at that time, so I began to explain to him why I had come. All of a sudden, the dust started up from the floor and we heard a dull explosion in the distance. He caught my eye and rolled his tongue round his dry mouth. At first he said nothing, the natural instinct of a man who has survived against the odds through the turbulent, sometimes terrible decades of Saddam's regime. His scholarship, safely focused on the glorious artefacts created when Baghdad was the centre of the Islamic world eight centuries ago, helped him to achieve a certain political invisibility. Then he looked me in the eye again and began to speak.

It's the British again. They have been bombing my family for over 80 years now. Four generations have lived and died with these unwanted visitors from Britain who come to pour explosives on us from the skies. It first began in 1920. My great grandfather, Abdul Rahman, was walking into our village for his last-born son's wedding when a two-winged plane suddenly came over the horizon and dropped a fireball amongst the celebrations. The guests were divided into separate areas for men and women, as they used to be in the villages in those days. The bomb fell on the men gathered inside, and killed or maimed half the men in our family—the firstborn son, three uncles, two cousins, four sons of my grandmother's father's brother. Since then, whenever it has suited them, the bombers come again.

Now their big brothers from America do most of it, but you can still see the RAF planes streaking across our skies flying their familiar routes, which they first charted in the 1920s. The flights began in earnest when they were preparing to leave finally (again) after the Second World War. They mapped our territory, laboriously, meticulously, took photographs of every square metre of our country. My cousin who studied there told me that at Keele University in England there are millions of reconnaissance photographs on microfilm of Iraq and Iran taken by RAF 680 Squadron before they left. You never know when we might need them, they said with a smile. When they look for oil, or decide to bomb us when they want to make sure they will have more of our oil for the future. Probably they still use them today when they sit in their operation rooms in England and plan which target amongst us to hit next.

Every square metre of our country photographed, from Al Basrah on the Gulf to Amādīyah in the mountains to the north. Our country! In a sense, though, it has hardly been our country at all—even if it has always been our land. Like most of the states in the Middle East it was invented by two men, one English, one French, during the First World War. Mark Sykes and François Georges-Picot were their names. You know, they just met up in

London and decided in secret between the two of them how it would all be. The defeated Ottoman Empire would be dismembered, and new colonies—Palestine, Transjordan, Iraq, Syria, Lebanon—simply invented out of the bits for the convenience of the two colonial powers that would rule them. The British, of course, already controlled Egypt and Sudan. Iraq was made out of three leftover *wilayat* of the Ottoman Empire. During the First World War the British promised the Kurds their own state, Kurdistan, the Arabs independence if they supported the British in attacking the Turks, which they did; but by 1923, the Brits had forgotten all about it. Along with the French they created vassal states for themselves that were no nations, just sets of lines drawn on the map according to their interests. Up till then, there had been no borders or boundaries between us all. The whole of the Empire was open from one end to the other—you could walk from al-Quds (Jerusalem) to İstanbul without a single frontier to cross. There were different regions, of course, ours was Upper and Lower Mesopotamia, as it always had been. Then their boundaries, drawn with their barbed wire, marked out their new 'protectorates', empty they said except for a few nameless tribesmen like my great-grandfather and grandfather who did not need to be consulted about what was good for them. Nomads have no rights. They are not really there at all, just like the peasant farmers of Palestine.

Not like the oil company that came quickly afterwards. Or the soldiers. Those French quickly landed their Senegalese troops in Beirut when the war ended and occupied the whole northern coastal area. The British used their Indian troops to invade Palestine, put in advisers elsewhere in Syria, and occupied the whole of Mesopotamia. All their Middle Eastern colonies in those days were run by Anglo-Indian administrations. They were not British colonies you know—they were 'dependencies of British India'.

He stopped for a moment, looked hard at the floor, and fell into silence. I offered him a cigarette. He smoked it for a while, watching the blue smoke rise to the ceiling.

'So what happened after they had taken over?' I asked. He breathed heavily, and shook his head.

Well. Between the two of them, they occupied the whole of the old territories of the Empire. At the same time, the British made several public statements to international forums that all 'liberated' territories would be governed on the principle of what they called the 'consent of the governed' by their own national administrations. The Arabs took them at their word: had they not already been induced to fight with the British against the Turks on that very promise? Remember that so-called Lawrence of Arabia they still make so much of? So, in March 1920, the General Syrian Congress in Damascus passed a resolution proclaiming independence for Syria, Palestine, and the Lebanon. Iraqi leaders immediately declared Iraq's independence too, with Amir Abdullah their king. Those British and French responded by going straight to the League of Nations, which obligingly gave them mandates over the whole territory. Not surprising, since they controlled it anyway. Mandate from whom? They said themselves that the term 'mandate' was just a piece of legal fiction to legitimate their new colonies.

We didn't just accept it though. King Faisal's troops attacked the French on the Lebanon border, the Arabs rebelled in Palestine, and our people of the Middle Euphrates rose against the British. The French responded by occupying the whole of Syria. In Iraq, the British didn't use their Indian troops: instead they used the newly formed Royal Air Force to bomb us. My great grandfather's wedding, remember? They had already tried out the RAF in Somaliland. In a two-month joint operation with the British Camel Corps they had overthrown the Dervish leader Mohammed bin Abdullah Hassan—whom the British characteristically called the 'Mad Mullah'. Mad because he wanted to get rid of them, of course. It was generally thought that the air force bombing and strafing against the nationalists had been the key to the operation's success.

Their new colonial secretary, Winston Churchill, he recognized early on the advantages of airpower for maintaining imperial control over his vast British territories. Before the uprising had even begun, he had enquired about the possibility of using airpower to take control of Iraq. This would involve, he said, using 'some kind of asphyxiating bombs calculated to cause disablement of some kind but not death...for use in preliminary operations against turbulent tribes'. You can't forget words like that. Nor the ones that followed. 'I do not understand this squeamishness about the use of gas,' he said. 'I am strongly in favour of using poison gas against uncivilized tribes.' So, after the Somaliland success, Churchill ordered a similar RAF operation in Iraq. The result was predictable. The rebellious Iraqis were also successfully 'pacified'. The British made war and called it peace. Does it make any difference for them? Churchill came to Cairo the next year, with his Lawrence of Arabia, for a conference on the future of the British mandates. No Arabs were invited. They installed Faisal, whom the French had thrown out of Syria, as King of Iraq. Despite fierce resistance in Baghdad, a plebiscite was arranged to vote him in.

Yes, the new RAF had been out to prove its use. It had only just been set up as a separate section of their armed forces. Anyone could see the advantages of technology like that for controlling far-away peoples. It was the future. Wing-Commander Sir Arthur Harris, that notorious 'Bomber Harris', put it this way: 'The Arab and Kurd now know what real bombing means in casualties and damage. Within 45 minutes a full-size village can be practically wiped out and a third of its inhabitants killed or injured.' Just 45 minutes a village—not bad. So the British established five RAF squadrons in Britain, five in Egypt, four in Iraq and in India, and one in the Far East. From now on we would never see their faces when we were fighting. Yes, after they had got rid of the Turks, when some of us had fought alongside them, they returned from the air like demons. For months RAF 30 Squadron flew over us, killing our men and our families until it was safe for the Indian soldiers and their British officers to set up their camps nearby. British control was restored.

I still have one of the propaganda photographs they produced at the time of our first 'liberation' from the Turks. It's a picture of the

'Peace Review'. This Peace Review was just the first, for another defeat and triumph followed—this time that of the British over the Iraqis. Look at that de Havilland 9 flying overhead, with its machine-gunner facing backwards ready to spray bullets on anyone below, with its 450 pounds of bombs tucked beneath its wings. Doesn't leave you many illusions about who is in charge. Power comes from above. Look.

He rummaged in his briefcase, took out an old, dog-eared postcard, and handed it to me (Figure 5). I peered at it for a while, trying to make it all out. From the shadows on the ground, it must have been late afternoon. A big circle of Arab spectators watching a military parade. In the centre, British officers standing opposite a line of ranked Camel Corps. Huge flags were flapping above

5. Peace review, Baghdad, 1918.

them, with an old two-winged aircraft flying prominently overhead. I could make out the French flag and the Union Jack.

'What's the flag at the front?' I asked.

It's the Italian navy ensign. They fought on the side of the British in that war, remember. Keep it! A souvenir, for you, to remember all this when you leave. They will only stay a while, my grandfather had heard. Indeed, they did go away eventually, in 1932, but as in Egypt, this did not mean that we became really independent. Some independence! We were made to sign a treaty in which we agreed to let Britain control our foreign policy, keep its two air bases at Habbaniyya near Baghdad and Shu'aiba near Basra, use Iraq freely for its troops in time of war, and maintain its complete monopoly of the Iraq Petroleum Company. It may have been called the Iraq Petroleum Company, but the British government controlled it. There was no Iraqi ownership at all. According to the independence treaty, the IPC was given exclusive exploration rights in Iraq. These were revoked in 1961, but the company itself did not come under Iraqi control until it was nationalized by Hasan al-Bakr and Saddam Hussein in 1972. That was a popular move. No wonder they don't like him! They want to get their oil back even now. They are already talking about which of their companies will get the rights to it when they have occupied our country again.

He smiled for a moment, and then sank back into his chair as if he were thinking ahead to the prospect of another occupation. He had stopped looking at me, and was going over it all in his mind, as if it were a story that, once started, he could not stop himself from telling right through to the end, however many times he would have to backtrack and retrace the pattern of its compulsive, sinuous repetitions.

So the British left, but only in name. We were to govern ourselves, we were told, under their guidance and control. Things came to a head during the Second World War, when many of us looked to the

Axis powers to deliver us from submission to Britain. When Prime Minister Rashid 'Ali al-Kailani got a bit awkward about giving permission for British troops to land in Iraq, they made it known that he would have to go, and he was forced to resign. Rashid 'Ali responded by organizing a *coup d'état* against the anglophile Prince Regent. The British refused to recognize his government, and demanded their right to more troop landings. Their commander at Habbaniyya then attacked Iraqi troops that had surrounded the base. Soon they occupied Basra, took Baghdad, and reinstated the Prince Regent on the throne. Their brute force had won control once more. Directed by the British Embassy, the new regime instituted a purge of the armed forces and government administration, and sent nationalist sympathizers for execution or to the Al-Faw detention camp. That's where they put my father, Abu Karim. He was in there all the time I was growing up as a young boy.

That cosy relationship between the British and their tame Iraqi dynasty (just like the one they had with the Shah of Persia and the King of Jordan, whom they'd also put on their thrones) continued right up to the Baghdad Pact in 1955, the last fawning agreement of a Hashemite monarch with the British. The next year it was Suez! The British were beaten! And before long, in 1958, there was a second army *coup d'état*, which brought the end of the hated Hashemite regime and British influence in Iraq. But not the end of British intervention. At first, we thought we had seen the last of them. No tame monarchy, no bases, no canal, but still getting the oil they wanted. Why would they ever come back? They had left with their tails between their legs, and the freed world had asserted itself at Bandung. But then they lost Iran too, and Saddam was encouraged to take them out. We were dying again. They were back.

Now they are saying that Iraq is 'a threat' to them. But hasn't it always been they who have threatened us? Oh yes, they certainly constitute a threat to us. They have been developing nuclear weapons since the 1940s. They were bombing us with chemicals long before then. It was Churchill himself who ordered the use of mustard gas against the Kurds in Northern Iraq in 1923, when they rebelled on hearing that the British had abandoned their promise of a Kurdish state. It took almost 18 months of repeated RAF attacks on the Kurdish city of Sulaimaniyya before they were finally repressed. Well, hardly finally. The RAF was bombing the Kurds again in 1931 when the British were preparing Iraq for 'independence', which they were about to grant without any reference to the special position of the Kurds in Iraq. You can still meet Kurds today who can remember being machine-gunned and bombed by the RAF in the 1920s. My friend Ibrahim was visiting the Korak mountains a while ago and came across an old man who could still recall it all. 'They were bombing here in the Kaniya Khoran,' he told him. 'Sometimes they raided three times a day.'

Yes, we are a threat to them, as that Tony Blair now tells his people, warning them of our 'weapons of mass destruction'. Every time we break bread, thousands of them are at risk from each bite that we take. Every time I chew a grape or a sugared date, suck a mulberry or an apricot, someone in England must shudder in fear. Every time my son climbs a tree to find a fig, the fine imperial gentlemen of England are put at risk. Yet all we have ever wanted to do is to live our own lives without them. The other night on TV I heard an old Iraqi saying, 'They have everything, we have nothing. We don't want anything from them—but they still want more from us.' All we ask is for them to stop interfering with us. We have not been bombing them since 1920. It is they who have been bombing us. Do they never think of that? It never bothers them. They seem to think of it as their God-given right. Or is it another of their human rights—the right to bomb? Not by our God, *alhamdo lillah*. Bombing us ever since their air force was formed, whenever they chose. And still they claim that it is we who are a threat to them. So much so that they have been killing us over the decades, bomb after bomb after bomb, whenever we displeased them or went against their interests. Our problem, though, I suppose, is that we have never been an easy catch. We didn't just go along with everything they wanted, like many countries in the Middle East. So they keep coming and bombing, but we keep slipping out of their grasp, again and again!

They will never subdue us, you will see, never 'pacify' us—even if they keep at it for all eternity.

It was a few years ago, in 1998, two days before Ramadan. My family were all sleeping in our flat in Baghdad, in the high apartment building that looks down Mansur St, towards Zawra' Park. A couple of hours before we were to rise for the *fajr*, the early-morning prayer, the sirens suddenly sounded and bombs began to fall around us, lighting the sky with their sinister firework explosions. The white powdery fronts of buildings and bridges were dropping away like sandcastles collapsing before the tide. Since then, and their invention of their 'no-fly zones', they have never really stopped. Except for when they vanish so that the Turks can fly in and bomb the Kurds—the very people that their no-fly zone is supposed to be protecting. The British themselves admit that they have bombed us at least once every other day over the past year. It is their longest bombing campaign since the Second World War. Now they say they are coming again, to destroy our families once more and to change our government just as they did so many times before. Why do they come out of the skies at us for so many years from so far away? Why are we of such interest to them? Because we have 'their' oil. That is the real threat that has never gone away, from 1920 until today.

I often wonder how they would feel if we had been bombing them in England every now and then from one generation to the next, if we changed their governments when it suited us, blockaded them, destroyed their hospitals, deprived them of clean water, and killed their children and their families. How many children is it that have died now? I can't even bring myself to think how many. They say that their imperial era is over now. It does not feel that way when you hear the staccato crack of their fireballs from the air. Or when the building shakes around you and your children from their bombs as you lie in your bed. It is then that you dream of real freedom—*in shaa' allah*—freedom from the RAF.

Chapter 5
Nomads, nation-states, borders

Despite nominal independence, many former colonies remain subject to neo-colonial (that is, continuing colonialism after independence) interference, invasion, subjection, and control of various kinds. Within the state, meanwhile, one of the most pressing issues has been the control of land. The problem of landlessness has long been a focus of political opposition and peasant unrest amongst those who make up the wretched of the earth. In Mexico, the politics of the Zapatista movement go back to the 1910 Zapatista revolution of the peasantry against the big landowners, the *hacendados*, who had expropriated their land. In Brazil, the Landless Workers Movement (MST), a mass social movement formed by rural workers in 1984, fights for land reform in a situation where 3 per cent of the population own two-thirds of cultivable land (1996 census—since then the disparity has increased). In India, peasant or tribal movements and rebellions, and acts of resistance against the *zamindari* landholding system, have continued uninterrupted from the colonial through the independence period, from the Gandhian Kisan peasant movement to the Maoist Naxalites.

The experience of dispossession and landlessness is particularly characteristic of settler colonialism. The South Africa Native Land Act of 1913 made it illegal for African people to possess or occupy land outside the 'Scheduled Native Areas', except as farm labourers. As a result, many lost their homes and means of subsistence. The effects of this continue today, with very little land redistribution achieved despite the promises of the ruling African National Congress party. In 1972 Aboriginals and Torres Strait Islanders established their famous 'Tent Embassy', a tin shack on the lawns of Capital Hill in Canberra, as a highly effective strategy to publicize their claim for land rights. The struggle for 'native title' has also been a major concern for native Americans in North America, for dispossessed African farmers in Zimbabwe who have campaigned for the basic land rights embodied in the Abuja Declaration, while dispossession from family land through force or the legal chicanery of the state and the claim for the right of return represents the central issue for Palestinians.

Nomads

Some indigenous people were city dwellers, some were farmers, some were nomadic people, grazing livestock. Sometimes they were both, settled but migrating periodically, according to the season. For colonizers coming from the West, they were often invisible, bizarre as that seems, or, more to the point, simply considered of no account. Settler colonialism was built on the fiction of an empty land, of 'a land without a people', a phrase which means a land with people who do not count, whose homes and land can be easily stolen and occupied.

Nomadic people in the Americas or Australasia never owned or possessed land in a European sense, which is how from the start European colonists were able, allegedly following the legal concept of property such as that of the 17th-century English philosopher John Locke, to declare the land empty, *'terra nullius'* or *'vacuum domicilium'*. It is for this reason that what is called 'native title' represents a claim of extraordinary complexity. At war, here, are not simply two peoples but different epistemologies or modes of thinking and conceptualization, where the European invokes a legal notion of individual property, ownership, and possession, that is fundamentally at odds with those societies that traditionally operate through communal systems where things are held in common, possessed exclusively by no one. Nomadic peoples work the land, have an intimate relation to it, but do not claim a possessive relation of ownership, seeing it rather as a resource for all the family or community, no different in that sense from the air or the sky. The relationship is a communal, sometimes an ancestral and sometimes a sacred one, known to and acknowledged by all without having to be written down.

The French philosophers Gilles Deleuze and Félix Guattari have conceptualized the process of the appropriation of land and its confiscation from those who have formerly worked it, with or without legal title, through the concepts of what they call 'territorialization' and 'deterritorialization'—terms which separate the stages of original occupation and subsequent dispossession. A third moment of 'reterritorialization' describes the violent dynamics of the colonial propagation of economic, cultural, and social transformation of the land and its indigenous culture, at the same time signalling the sometimes-successful process of resistance to deterritorialization through anti-colonial movements. Other forms of resistance have developed in the postcolonial era: combative negotiation with the state for rights to land, as in the case of the Australian Indigenous land rights movements, or the Brazilian MST, or even, as has happened in the American Midwest, the simple repurchase of lands which had been appropriated as part of the homesteading colonization of the land by settlers in the 19th century, but which are now being abandoned as virtually worthless because the land itself is not fertile enough for modern intensive agricultural farming.

Deleuze and Guattari have further developed the idea of the nomad as a strategic concept, using the term for the person who most effectively resists the controlling institutions of the modern state, which is based on the assumption that its citizens will and must be settled. Any account of the Roma (also known as gypsies) or 'travellers' in Europe, from Ireland to Spain to Switzerland to Hungary to Romania, will provide graphic instances of the ways in which the state has regarded those whose life involves a permanent state of migrancy as a serious social threat that requires heavy-handed intervention, management, control—or, in the case of the Nazis, extermination.

Nomadism, the practice of movement across territories, Deleuze and Guattari argue, operates as a form of lateral resistance through borders in acts of defiance of assertions of hegemonic control by the state. The idea of nomadism, they suggest, can be extended to include all forms of cultural and political activity that transgress or dissolve the boundaries of contemporary social codes or intellectual disciplines. Nomadism, however, cannot be celebrated simply as an anti-capitalist strategy, for the simple reason that enforced nomadism is also one brutal characteristic mode of capitalism itself, which historically has precipitated mass migrations and continues to do so. For centuries capitalism has profited from the closure of land and resulting coerced movement of its inhabitants, now transformed into migrant workers, to the cities, where, even in some of the richest countries, homeless people can be found sleeping on the streets. In colonial and postcolonial history, nomads have not just been those who still live in a pre-capitalist mode of subsistence: in the past two centuries, nomadism has been a state of existence forced upon millions by capitalism. Landlessness constitutes a central problem not just for many peasant communities around the world, but also for the unprecedented seventy million people worldwide who have been forced from their homes by war, loss of land, or simple poverty, to become homeless and sometimes stateless.

Nation-states

One major effect of colonialism in its various forms was to export and settle millions of Europeans in the Americas, Africa, Australasia, and the Middle East, and thereby produce a long-term reorganization of the populations of the world. A second enduring effect of colonial rule was the institution of the British and French legal systems as the permanent basis of world economic and political governance. A third consequence of colonial rule would ultimately be the reorganization of the whole world from empires into nation-states.

The nation-state, a form of political organization implying various obligations of states to their citizens, and the rights of the citizen in relation to the state, was a concept fundamental to European 17th- and 18th-century political thought. The very first nation-state, the Netherlands, was created from a former colony of Spain, thereby instituting its political form as the fundamental decolonizing option. The nation-state is defined not by its sovereign but by its particular people—who, in its idealized form, possess a common language, culture, religion, and race or ethnicity, living within demarcated, recognized borders. It is, in a sense, a tribe writ large, bound together not by the bonds of family, but by some or all of those other features held in common. In practice, however, no nation-states have been able to claim such homogeneity. It has therefore been necessary to standardize, and to expel: the nation-state is not natural, it has to be created. In the case of the original European nation-states such as the Netherlands or France, this process could take centuries. While state schooling could eventually engineer something like a common language (it was, remarkably, only after 1870 that the majority of French people spoke French), colonization enabled the export of surplus populations of those who did not belong on account of their ethnic or religious identity, or simply their class (i.e. their poverty), to settler colonies outside Europe. Today the process has been reversed: newer nation-states export migrants legally or illegally to the West. With the creation of nation-states out of the break-up of the Hapsburg Empire at the end of the First World War, millions of Europeans were relocated to their alleged 'home' country elsewhere, even if they had never been there. This key mechanism of the establishment of the nation-state would be formalized in the 20th century through the mechanism of partition, whereby new states (Ireland, Turkey/Greece with reduced borders, India/Pakistan, Israel/Palestine) were created through the forced expulsion of millions of people to their 'own' countries.

Unsettled states: nations and their borders

The modern passport, a necessity for those who wish to cross the borders of nation-states, was also created after the First World War as part of the same process of the reinvention of the political map as a bundle of nation-states. Notwithstanding the claims for the cultural identity of its people, nothing really defines a nation like its borders; the modern idea and often brutal reality of the international border paradoxically marks the core of the nation-state. There are some 'nations' without physical borders, such as the first nations of Canada (a title chosen by indigenous North Americans for themselves, in preference to the usual term for indigenous 'fourth world' peoples). For the most part, however, the border creates and marks the limit of the nation, and produces the space in which the nation's infrastructional machinery, its government, its tax collectors, can operate. Unlike empires, which functioned with a relatively relaxed concept of sovereignty and whose borders were often indistinct, the nation defines itself by its borders, with the result that the world is full of sovereignty disputes over tiny pieces of land or islands, claimed by sometimes two or three nation-states: on all maps of India, for example, you will read the legend: 'The Government of India states that "the external boundaries of India are neither correct nor authenticated"'. Six countries claim the Spratly Islands in the South China Sea, which are uninhabited and mostly reefs lying submerged beneath the water. The nation is a kind of voracious bureaucratic corporation. Its policed or militarized border serves to require other nations to recognize its autonomy, so that it can participate in the global community of nations. A community without communal values other than self-interest.

The territory of the earth is a mosaic of nations: or is it simply a mosaic of states? What makes a state a nation? Does it need to be one? A fundamental problem for the state, unless it possesses a monarch or emperor endowed with divine authority, is the question of what legitimates its authority. As the French proposed in 1789, the abstract idea of 'the people' fulfils this function in an ideal way. The nation becomes an empty space in which all forms of potential identification can be filled: race, religion, language, culture, history, the land: what makes you a part of your nation? You don't have to answer that question: you are part of a nation-state whether you like it or not. Unless you have been deemed not to be. Or unless you live at the border: literally on the peripheries between two countries, or between two cultures, languages, genders, histories. That is where decolonial border thinking can be found.

It always used to be assumed that in order to become a nation, its people should resemble each other as closely as possible, according to one or more of the characteristics outlined above. If some people looked different, spoke a different language, followed a different religion (or, worse, a different sect within the same religion), then this was considered a threat to what the political theorist Benedict Anderson has characterized as the 'imagined community' of the nation. Many people, languages, cultures have been—and are being—repressed by nation-states for this reason. The United States, a nation of immigrants, makes an interesting test case in its attempt to deal with this problem of how to make the many one. First of all, everyone in the US has something in common, that they or their ancestors came as immigrants from somewhere else—though awkwardly this does not apply to the first nations of native Americans who were displaced or exterminated in order to make room for the new arrivals. Second, unlike most countries, more like an old dynastic empire in fact, even the landmass of the US does not form a cohesive unit, but is dispersed with other countries and oceans in between. In the absence of traditional links to land, history, and culture, and without an official religious identity since it was established as a secular state in order to provide religious freedom, the US creates its national identity through its political and economic system (democracy, free enterprise capitalism), its claim to political freedom, its flag, and any perceived global threats to this, from communists to Mexican immigrants. A succession of enemies has served to make all its different people feel collectively threatened, and therefore to bond with each other.

The common values and material uniformity of American life are such that since the 1960s minorities have been permitted to proclaim the 'difference' of their identities and thus not to aspire to become altogether 'one' at every level. Such hyphenated identities are the mark of the enduring social differences produced by race and racial prejudice. While ever-increasing disparity of wealth has been one of the results of the introduction of neo-liberal economic policies since the 1980s, that kind of difference has never been a problem for a nation's identity. Despite the fact that from a traditional nationalist point of view, many US Americans have very little in common other than being defined by their current citizenship, place of residence, and diversity, the US approach to the creation of national identity has been very successful. It does permit certain kinds of difference. The mistake of the postcolonial state has often been to take the Romantic account of the nation, first formulated by the German philosopher Johann Gottfried Herder, and developed to an extreme at state level by Nazi Germany, as the only possible way in which a nation can be constructed: a holistic people with a common language, history, culture, and race. Though this model also worked well as an idea for constructing a sense of solidarity and a goal for which people were fighting in the anti-colonial movements, the attempt to stabilize it and impose it by means of state control after independence has in general had disastrous consequences. Despite its consistent critique of the conceptual construction of the nation and internationalist theoretical orientation, postcolonialism itself has been appropriated in the name of a variety of contemporary cultural nationalisms (e.g. by some in China or India).

The Hindutva movement in India, based on the ideology of a return to the authenticity of the golden age, of 'the wonder that was India', and its attachment to lands that are peopled by minorities who wish to be independent (India administered Kashmir, obviously, but also those 'restricted areas' disallowed in all foreigners' tourist visas, for example, the huge salient of north-east India), has been the most recent national movement to pursue the illusions of national homogeneity derived from 19th-century Germanic ideas of authenticity. If you doubt the link, ask why newly printed copies of Hitler's *Mein Kampf* can be found for sale on street bookstalls all over northern India. The project of the quest for authentic Indian-ness, for a *Hindu Rasthra*, an ethnically pure Hindu nation, which will eliminate or exclude minorities such as Muslims or Christians, and fix Dalits (untouchables) and Adivasis (tribals) into its eternal racial hierarchy of caste, has now come to power in the shape of the BJP government. The Hindutva movement mimics the history of its neighbour Sri Lanka, which fought a thirty-year civil war as a result of the 'Sinhala only' movement that was initiated against the (now defeated) Tamil minority after S. W. R. D. Bandaranaike's general election victory in 1956. People in the West always assume that the Western system of democracy must be the best political system for all countries of the world. However, in countries with well-defined, different ethnic groups, where one is in the large majority, such as Sri Lanka, democracy can become a form of popular tyranny and oppression. In such countries, the minority have no legitimate political means of resistance against the tyranny of the majority should they choose to oppress them.

These repressive nationalist projects are not necessarily generated internally, however: nationalism, as Benedict Anderson has suggested, is often the creation of those who have left the country, and who, in safe and prosperous exile, fondly fund at long distance future recreations of idealized memories of their past. Is it the diasporic spread of a people beyond its borders that creates the nation? These nostalgic cultural imaginings are an effect of globalization, produced from afar by those who now never have to encounter the nation's everyday realities. Money from non-residents creates the link between the idealized past and its violent production by state governments and non-governmental organizations in the present. The racism and intolerance to which such holistic conceptions of the nation almost inevitably lead means that postcolonial intellectuals have tried to think of the nation differently, to propose alternative conceptions which begin not with an idealized version of how it might be, but with how it is in reality—very often a country of many languages, ethnicities, religions, with a great variety of people living in its margins and peripheries. As the Indian critic Leela Gandhi has argued, different forms of community to the nation can and have been imagined. The postcolonial nation does not have to require identity from its population: the city provides a far more constructive model of possibility—the greatest cities of the world typically are those with the greatest diversity. Take London or New York, where people of different faiths and ethnicities negotiate their lives in harmony with each other. Why should it be so different for nation-states?

The idea and ideal of the nation is often imaged as a woman, and the ideology of nationalism often invests the nation's core identity with an idealized, patriarchal image of ideal womanhood, a construction critically analysed in Rabindranath Tagore's 1916 novel *Home and the World* (*Ghôre Baire*). When this happens, women effectively have no nation: 'As a woman my country is the whole world' claimed Virginia Woolf in 1938. Throughout the 20th century, women have striven to resist patriarchal nationalism by forming community and transnational organizations. The uprising that was to topple the Russian Czar in 1917 began with demonstrations on International Women's Day. The great English suffragette Sylvia Pankhurst was affiliated to the First International Working Women's Congress held in Moscow in 1920. The homogeneous nation is an ideal as patriarchal as that of state imperialism. Transnational movements and links between resistance movements have been among the most effective responses to patriarchal nationalism and imperialism since the end of the 19th century, since resistance to the oppression of the colony or the nation can best be initiated by cutting through its restrictive boundaries and reaching out beyond them.

While some nations try to sweep away their fragments, others are invented out of fragments: Indonesia, for example, was created by the Dutch, the Japanese, and the Javanese from uncontainable diversity that still threatens to tear it apart. Other nations live and die every day as fragments: take Palestine. The map of Palestine (Figure 6) after the 1993 Oslo Agreement looks like the night sky on a cloudy night. Whereas the stars have space between them, and the thousands of Indonesian islands have sea, Palestine has military checkpoints and Israeli-controlled territory in-between its stars on its map. Since 1993, Israel has illegally placed more and more fortified Jewish settlements all over the West Bank in order to populate it with Israelis, lay claim to the land taken from Jordan, and ensure that there will never be an independent Palestinian state.

Could the ever-more fragmented bits and pieces that make up the Palestinian zones of the Occupied Territories ever seriously comprise a nation, a state, a homeland? This map vividly recalls other maps of an earlier colonial regime: the Bantustans, the tiny so-called independent homelands allocated to black South Africans during the apartheid era. Ultimately, even if it takes a very long time, annexation of the West Bank will eventually result in Israel integrating the Palestinian population as citizens. In the end, history tells us that artificial divisions instituted between people who live in the same place always break down, one way or another.

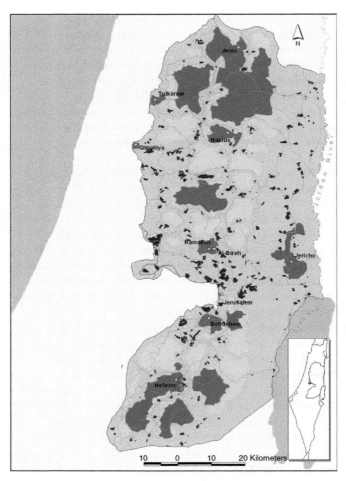

6. 'Palestine Bantustan': map of the West Bank after the Oslo Agreement.

The wall

Nation-states rely on cohesive borders: the border *is* the nation-state. If borders are open, permeable, then the nation's peoples cannot be controlled. They may leave, others may enter illicitly: migrants, immigrants, undesirables. In practice, the modern state functions by means of a deliberate contradiction: a combination of strict border controls together with tolerance, even at times quiet encouragement, of illegal immigration—by workers who then have no rights and can be paid less.

Walls function in two ways: there can be walls designed to keep people from coming in, such as the Great Wall of China, built to keep the Mongols out. Hadrian's Wall, built by the Romans to keep out the Picts. The Great Hedge of India, grown from Leia in the Punjab to the south of Burhanpur on the Maharashtran border to enforce the British Salt Tax that was to be challenged by Gandhi's Salt March in 1930. The rabbit-proof fence in Australia, built to keep rabbits from migrating and stolen Aboriginal children from returning home across the countryside. And, since 2006, the wall being built across the US-Mexican border to keep out Mexican and other migrants.

They are the walls that stretch through the countryside or zigzag across the city, built as border fences to keep people and things out. The limits of liberalism. To defend the state.

Walls can also divide cities as well as countries—the Berlin Wall, built to keep people in; the Green Line that winds its way through Nicosia to keep the Cypriot people apart. Or sometimes cities are surrounded by walls, especially those at the pressure points of direct contact between the first and third worlds, such as Ceuta and Melilla, the two Spanish colonies on the North African mainland. Like Martinique in the Caribbean, they are part of the European Union. With funds from the EU, the two cities are surrounded by a 10-foot-high fence, with double razor-wire, electronic sensors, and infra-red cameras on top. Still the migrants, from Morocco, Algeria, and especially West Africa, try to climb in. Many of them are unaccompanied children. Rather than risk being entangled in the razor-wire of the fence, others pay large sums of money to risk a journey on rickety boats known as *pateras* to sail the 9-mile stretch across the treacherous waters to Spain, or they travel to Libya and pay for a passage to Malta or one of the closest Italian islands such as Lampedusa. No one knows how many drown, but they are numbered in their thousands, every year.

The separation walls of the West Bank, threading around cities and cutting through Palestinian farms, to keep the illegal Israeli settlers apart from the Palestinians, are designed as much to keep the Palestinians in as to keep them out of the illegal settlements and the 1948 state of Israel. Try visiting Bethlehem to experience what it is like. While Christians piously sing about the 'little town' every Christmas, 'How still we see thee lie | Above thy deep and dreamless sleep | The silent stars go by . . .', and millions of Christmas cards portray it in idyllic images, the actual town of Bethlehem is surrounded by an 8- to 9-metre high separation wall, with one entrance/exit, turned into a ghetto and a city-prison at once. The British street artist Banksy's The Walled-Off Hotel, built on Caritas Street near Manger Square where Christ is popularly believed to have been born, and looking right on to the wall, makes the point bluntly. But even Banksy, who remarked that Bethlehem is the 'least Christmassy place on earth', was able in December 2017 to team up with film director Danny Boyle to create an 'Alter-nativity' outside his hotel: in the film, we see local Palestinian children singing Jingle Bells under fake snow while the lofty grey concrete wall looms up right behind them.

Touch of evil

Tijuana, Mexico, is a city that has founded its relative prosperity on being a border town. The long street lines of the Avenida

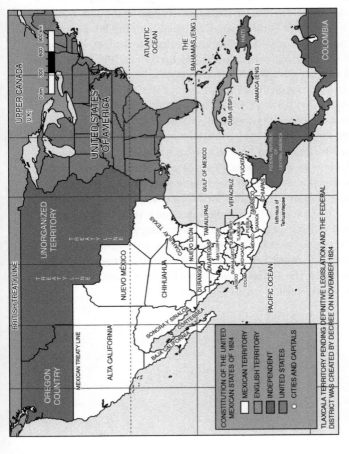

7. Mexico in 1824.

Revolucion could be anywhere in the US. Only the colours give it away: compared to the pastels of California, they are wildly out of control. At the main intersection, the yellow and red of the Sara store faces the sky blue of the Lobster Club, which looks on to the bright purple of the Bar, Grill, Dance, opposite the pink and red of Le Drug Store. Any language but Spanish for this border town, a town turned inside out. Outside the city, late at night, young men, prospective migrants, gather by the River Levy. With his promise of a border wall, US President Trump has become identified with a crack-down on illegal migrants from Mexico, but he is certainly not the first US president to focus on this issue. Operation Gatekeeper was the brainchild of President Bill Clinton in 1994, and for a while was claimed to be successful at keeping Mexicans out, its closed doors producing what was called (after the pinball machine game) the Banzai Run. Migrants ran head-on into the traffic on Interstate 5 to avoid border control—it was simply so dangerous that the guards would not chase them. Or they swam the Rio Grande to be picked up and roughed up at gunpoint by local vigilante patrols in Texas. These were, and are, people slipping across into a land that was once part of Mexico (Figure 7), forcibly annexed by the US in 1845, from which they are now excluded. The busiest section of the border is called Imperial Beach.

Chapter 6
Hybridity

While states have created more and more frontiers between peoples, migration across borders continues at an unprecedented rate and has already transformed the world. One of the most obvious effects of this aspect of globalization has been that cultures have become increasingly heterogeneous and diversified. It used to be thought, as we have seen, that individual cultures should be singular, complete, uniform like a single organism, with any extraneous elements removed. Everyone should speak the same language, practise the same religion, play the same games, eat the same cuisine, and have the same cultural interests and values if they were going to take on the identity of the country of which they were citizens. If you shared any of these characteristics with neighbouring countries, you would attempt to give your version a distinctive twist, emphasizing the differences, say, between American and British English ('two countries separated by a common language' as the Irish author George Bernard Shaw is reported to have quipped). This unity of culture was always an ideal, but it was certainly possible to travel in the 1950s from country to country and feel that you were entering distinctive, defined cultural realms. Of course there had always been immigration, but at that time the assumption was that immigrants would always assimilate into the dominant culture, and many in fact made strenuous efforts to do so, if not for themselves, then for their children. The same mind-set operated for race: in Australia, until 1973, immigration was limited to whites, and the government even made efforts to turn Aboriginal peoples into white people by eugenic methods of cross-breeding. These ideas first began to be challenged in the 1960s, particularly around the Civil Rights movement in the USA, when African-Americans campaigned not only for their political rights but also for recognition of their own identity and cultural values. This marked the beginning of a challenge to the politics of what has come to be known as cultural hybridity since it involved a refusal of assimilation to the values of white culture and a reversal of hierarchies: the transformation of Blackness into an icon of the beautiful, and the use of the term 'African-American', in which the African was foregrounded over the American.

In itself, the idea of cultural hybridity could nevertheless be seen as an expansion of W. E. B. Du Bois' concept of 'double consciousness' that was discussed above. In the context in which Du Bois was writing, double consciousness was the particular burden that the African-American had to bear in his or her particular society. On the other hand, more positively, we can see that however painful it might be as a state of mind, historically that disruptive dialectic has also formed the basis of the extraordinary cultural creativity of African-American people in the United States. African-Americans willed the negative into a positive. Drawing on the cultural memory of their own African heritage, African-Americans have adapted and transformed aspects of the European culture that they encountered in the United States. Nowhere is this more obvious than in the realm of music. The many different forms of African-American music— blues, funk, hip-hop, house, jazz, rhythm and blues, rag-time, rap, rock, soul—all emerged from the use of polyrhythmic structures of western and southern African dance and folk music that were combined with elements of English and Irish folk music, music hall songs, the new instruments and recording technologies available, and no doubt much else, to produce the distinctive African-American musical styles. Any consideration of

African-American music as a field illuminates the creative potential of mixing different cultural elements together rather than isolating them into single, distinct traditions.

African-American music has provided a model of culture in which mixture, rather than originality and 'authentic' pure forms, overtakes the exclusionary nationalist cultural dream to create new forms of identity. If this had happened in the USA since the 19th century, postcolonial critics recognized that it was taking place in a comparable way at many other places in the world where colonialism and migration had been, or were, bringing about the mixture of different cultures into new creative forms (the academic version of this would be the current stress on interdisciplinary work, despite the institutional division of universities into separate disciplines). The contradiction of the nationalist cultural ideal was that its accompanying dream of colonial empires always had the effect of diversifying the national culture rather than unifying it: 'ambivalence', wrote Frantz Fanon in 1952, is 'inherent in the colonial situation'. In the 1980s, the Indian critic Homi K. Bhabha published a number of influential essays showing how the British in India repeatedly experienced the challenge of the transformation of their own cultural values when encountering the diverse cultures of India. Bhabha, together with the Indian novelist Salman Rushdie, then demonstrated how this was happening in London in their own time in reverse: the immigrants were revolutionizing English culture at home. The word that they used to describe this process was 'hybridity'—a technical term originally used to describe the practice of cross-fertilizing two different species of plant, which had then been extended in the 19th century to philological accounts of mixed languages and from there to racial theory to describe the effects of cross-breeding between different so-called races in humans. Bhabha used this term, with the closely related concept of ambivalence, to emphasize that in considering the historical juxtapositions of different cultures he was not simply talking about a process of fusion, where different elements merge with each other. His interest was in moments of cultural untranslatability, where incompatible elements from different cultures collide with and against each other: it is at that moment, he suggests, quoting Rushdie, that 'newness enters the world'. We find a similar argument made by the Martiniquan poet Édouard Glissant, who uses the terms 'creolité' and 'opacity' to characterize the diversity, openness, and productive interrelationality of Caribbean cultures in contrast to what he regards as the essentialism of the Négritude movement initiated in the 1930s by two extraordinary poet-politicians, the Martiniquan Aimé Césaire and the Senegalese Léopold Senghor. Hybridity, in other words, is a theory of cultural creativity, in which the clash of incompatible entities generates entirely new forms.

The first person to discuss the creative dimensions of this practice was the Cuban anthropologist Fernando Ortiz, who in 1940 published *Cuban Counterpoint: Tobacco and Sugar*, in which he traced the processes of what he called 'transculturation', a concept which he invented as an antithesis to the then-standard sociological description of acculturation or cultural assimilation by immigrants. Ortiz showed how tobacco and sugar created by African slaves who performed the labour that produced the goods which flowed from the Cuban factories produced a local culture in which the different elements of black and white (tobacco/sugar, Africans/Spanish) developed a contrapuntal dialectic in relation to each other, transforming the cultures of the old and new worlds. In this brilliant book, Ortiz demonstrates how through their initial gift of cigars to the Spanish, the indigenous Caribs radically transformed the social practices of the whole world. He suggests that there was something radical in the doubled nature of this gift: 'In the fabrication, the fire and spiralling smoke of a cigar there was always something revolutionary, a kind of protest against oppression, the consuming flame and the liberating flight into the blue of dreams'.

Contrary to others of his time, Ortiz was always concerned to emphasize the African element in Cuban culture, the ways in which black mixed with white, especially in music as in the United States. To see how that process of hybridization of elements from different cultures works in practice, let's consider a more contemporary example—Algerian Raï.

Raï and Islamic social space

After the traumatic experiences of the Algerian War of Independence—the widespread torture of men, women, and children; the million-and-a-half Algerians killed by the French in their desperate attempt to retain their own privileges won by brutal military conquests in the 19th century, to maintain their occupation of a land whose diverse indigenous people were never subdued—the emergence of raï music in Algeria in the 1970s was a particularly heartening phenomenon. Raï is often described as raw, rough, earthy (*trab*): it is also defiant, assertive, passionate. The singers throw themselves at its rhythms with an unimaginable intensity that gives raï its unique energizing passion.

Raï music has been described as a product of the contradictory conditions of postcoloniality, produced in the precarious fissures of repeated paradoxical situations. The ethnomusicologist Philip V. Bohlman describes it as follows:

> Popular musicians sing against the institutions of the politically powerful, yet depend upon the connections of such institutions to the former colonizing nations, especially the recording industries of Paris and London. Popular music mobilizes the voiceless, but when the voiceless turn to Islam to enhance their mobilization, they cannot at the same time embrace popular music. Popular music enters the North African metropolis from the peripheries of tradition, but must sacrifice the past to enter the public sphere at the centre of urban society.

Raï has always been mobile and shifting as it changes its functions and locations, its instruments and its audiences. Its production is often casual and can be adapted easily according to specific needs. Its impromptu nature means that it never becomes fixed, that it always remains flexible and able to incorporate new contradictory elements.

Raï music began during the explosive population growth of the first generation of Algerians born after the end of the Algerian War of Independence in 1962. It came into its own in the late 1970s when singers, such as Sahraoui and Fadela, and Cheb Khaled, began to produce their own dynamic form of raï that drew on some of the sounds and rhythms of Western rock while reminiscent in its haunting self-expression of reggae and African-American blues. The emergence of raï is also associated with the migration of Algerians to the cities, and in that sense marks the appearance of a syncretic musical form that epitomizes the economic imperatives of modernity on its disenfranchised people. This involved much more than transactions of fusion, synthesis, or intermixture. People and cultures do not flow unimpeded and unchanged in the way that capital does. The social production of raï was not a single process, but rather involved histories of contested relations at every level of its production and consumption in Algerian society. To that extent, raï can work too as a broader metaphor for thinking about the complex relations of cultures to the forces of modernity.

As a musical form, raï originally developed soon after independence in the cosmopolitan port city of Wahrān (Oran), in western Algeria, where the young *chebs* (male singers such as Cheikh Meftah and Cheikh Djelloul Remchaoui) or *chabas* (women singers), singing in cabarets or at weddings, created new songs marked by radically honest lyrics about their own contemporary political and cultural situations. The titles *cheb/chab* that the performers were given, or gave themselves, marked their difference from traditional singers, suggesting their youthful audience, their lower social and artistic status, as well as signalling their innovative modern musical style.

Raï drew on the more modern *wahrāni* music already developed in the cities since the 1930s from the *malhūn*, vernacular sung poetry originally performed by Moroccan working-class artisans, and *andalus*, the classical city music of North Africa that originated out of the music of Al-Andalus in Muslim Spain. *Wahrāni* music had already begun the process of transforming traditional Arabic musical forms to the demands of modern mass-produced music and electric instruments, beginning with the accordion, absorbing influences from Moroccan (*chaabi*) and Egyptian (especially from Umm Kulthum, *Kawkab al-Sharq*, the 'Star of the East') dance and wedding music. This was combined with elements of Western rock, disco, and jazz, together with West African music, and songs from further afield such as Latin America and Bollywood—a range of sources that has no formal limits.

Hybridity

Musically, raï was also in part adapted from the songs sung by the *shīkhs* in the *badawi*, or traditional Bedouin tradition, as well as from the songs of the transgressive and vibrant woman singers, the *shīkhas*, who catered to the masculine spaces of the public bars and brothels of pre-independence Algeria, performing also at weddings, parties, and even religious festivals. The great Cheikha Remitti, generally accorded the title 'The Queen of Raï', began as, and in spirit has always remained, a *shīkha*, as her title suggests. Some women raï singers, on the other hand, started out as *maddāhas*, women poets who sing both religious and profane songs at gatherings exclusively for women at events such as circumcisions or *mendhis* prior to weddings. Raï performers originally began by using distinctive local acoustic instruments—string instruments such as the *oud* (the Arabic lute); wind instruments such as the *gaṣba* and *nāy*, throaty haunting reed flutes; percussion instruments such as the *banndīr* (tambourine), *gallāl* (drone), *qarqabu* (castanet), *darbūka*, *ṭbal*,

83

and *ṭbila* (drums); together with the violin, accordion, and trumpet. From the earliest days, however, some musicians, such as the Qada and the Baba brothers, adapted their material for Western electronic instruments and created 'electric' raï. In a similar way at the level of language, raï is sung in the local dialect, but a dialect that is inflected with running allusions and streetwise borrowings from local Spanish, French, and Jewish dialects.

The development of raï was also precipitated by technological change: in some respects, it rose in its modern form in response to the specific demands of the local cassette-recording industry after the end of the vinyl record. The invention of cassettes for the first time put local entrepreneurs in control of music production, and much of raï's international success is owed to the producers and middlemen in Algeria and then France who imposed their own needs and preferences in the recording studio on to the musical forms. It was never an 'authentic' music outside these motors of production; it developed through being played increasingly on radio stations abroad, primarily in Morocco and France. Although these commercialized conditions have been criticized in Algeria, this new situation allowed the music to emerge as an independent form and force, breaking established conventions within the musical and social culture of Algeria. It has always been, literally and metaphorically, multi-track.

The term 'raï' literally means 'an opinion', 'a point of view', 'a way of seeing things'; it can also mean 'an aim'. In terms of asserting its own perspectives, its own subversive will-to-power, therefore, raï encapsulates many of the qualities that are fundamental to postcolonial and decolonial perspectives. Beginning as the expression of those who found themselves on the periphery, immigrants to the cities who lived in deprived conditions of poverty, poor housing, and unemployment, raï's musical culture was quickly transformed out of the margins into the major popular expression for young people of social conditions within Algerian society. The speed with which raï spread across Algeria and North Africa was testimony to the degree to which it provided points of recognition that had never previously been articulated. It became quickly identified with 'the word of the people' (*shaab*). Raï's appeal lay in its recompositions of recognizable but destructured elements through mass-produced popular modes from the perspective of those at the social fringes. Raï singers took elements from a wide range of existent cultural forms—sacred, secular, classical, popular—and represented them in ways that took them out of their conventional contexts into new kinds of cultural expression. In invoking a range of complex cultural codes in forms that allowed spontaneous invention and elaboration, raï singers were able to express their own relations of contradiction and ambivalence towards the society around them, which was at once rapidly changing in economic terms and caught within rigid social structures. Raï stands in the highly contested space between modern interpretations of what constitute traditional Muslim values, and the traditional responses of accommodation and resistance to forces of historical change by Muslim societies.

Raï did not necessarily offer an explicit way forward in political or ideological terms. Rather, it represented the emotional expression of those who found themselves at the points of disruption within Algerian society and on the wrong side of its practices of legitimation. Raï's popularity can be seen as a mark of its success in providing forms of identification to which many could immediately respond, particularly the *hittistes* ('those who prop up the wall'), whose primary adult experience was one of unemployment, boredom, and disillusion with the government. In political terms, raï, like many postcolonial cultural forms, was first of all concerned to articulate problems and situations, as a necessary first stage before moving towards any possible resolutions.

A hybrid genre of this kind says something about contemporary social problems, social contradictions: its politics are in its articulations, even in its articulations of inarticulate states of being or non-being—it has no quick solutions, and may well have no immediate solutions at all. Like postcolonialism itself, it offers challenges or questions before solutions, and allows its audiences to develop and interpret what Homi K. Bhabha called a 'third' space, outside the already-thought with relevant new meanings of their own. It does not arrive delivering its meaning fully-formed— rather it enables new meanings to be created and projected in the space of dialogic encounters. Because it articulates the raw, the rough, the vulgar, social, and sexual tensions in a changing, torn social milieu that no longer adds up to a coherent civil society, it has often been criticized for its lack of respectability, for the impurity of its politics—as well as, in the case of raï, for the profanity of its language. For this reason, raï is also credited with, or criticized for, its disruptive, destabilizing effects on its listeners as well as its performers—in other words, for producing the very effects that it names.

الغضب الراي ، جعلتني أغير طرقي. جعلتني أخسر منزلي

Angry raï made me change my ways, it made me lose my home
(Cheb Khaled, 'Nti, nti')

Clearly what raï does do is encourage forms of self-expression and identification in ways that, in musical terms, replicate some of the social tensions that it enunciates, particularly in the subversive borrowings from the traditional *shīkhs* set against electric sounds taken from commercial Western rock, which express ambivalence between traditional cultural forms and simultaneous aspirations towards Western cultures. At the same time, it continues to refuse the West by maintaining the distinctive fluid tonal sounds and rhythms of Arab music: whereas Western music, for example, is restricted to half tones by its notation system and harmonic scales, Arab music does not limit itself to set intervals, and freely moves across its various augmented scales. Its rhythms flow in an equally resourceful pattern set against the beat—only jazz since the 1950s can compare to the musical inventiveness of this music, called into being by the extempore creativity of the performing musician.

In the same way, the singer's lyrics will forge traditional lines and refrains with references that incorporate the particular social world of his or her audience. By articulating within the songs recognizable local topics and cryptic allusions to places of transgressive love, such as the forest, as well as to the family and the sacred, raï forges a medium that speaks specifically to everyday forms and difficulties of Maghrebian experience, while itself being given meanings within the contexts of contemporary social life that are enacted through the performance. Raï does not represent either a search for, or a creation of, a new cultural identity. It is rather part of a process in which novel kinds of perceptions relating to cultural identity are staged, debated, and negotiated in challenging ways that were not previously possible.

From the mid-1980s raï achieved a wide following across the Maghreb as well as in North African communities in France, Spain, and elsewhere. It was one of the first examples of so-called 'world music'. This concept, which emerged in the late 1980s, is often described in terms of 'fusion': of Western elements, of rock and jazz, with the tonal harmonics, rhythms, and particular sounds of local music. Fusion marks a phenomenon of globalization in which the cultural channels of communication have been opened for all by technology, which intersects different musical sounds with ease—quite literally, in fact, on the synthesizer. In some cases, the simple idea that these elements have bonded together into new mixed modes may well be accurate, though it is notable that some raï songs, such as Haïm's 'Wahlaich', were simultaneously produced in Arab and French versions, and fusion did not prevent the development of very specific local forms. The sound of the band Raïna Raï, who come from Algiers, for example, is distinctly different from the traditional earthy or popular forms of raï that first emerged along the Wahrān coastline.

In contrast to its varied and ambivalent role in Algerian society, in its presentation to the West, raï has been brought in to tell a familiar story—the story that the West always wants to hear about other cultures that appear to operate according to norms significantly different to its own, and which resist accommodation and incorporation into Western economic and ideological models. As reported in the French and world press, raï has been turned into a Western-style Algerian youth revolt, and presented as a second, postcolonial war of liberation and modernity against paternalist tradition, a revolution against the social rigidities and disparities of wealth under the current Algerian regime, and as a secularist revolt by Algerian youth against the strictures of Islamism in Algeria, breaking social and religious taboos on sexuality, alcohol, and drugs. Raï singers have been profiled as bohemian rebels who aspire to express a free individualism that emulates the commercial individualism of the West and allies them to international pop icons of rebellion such as James Dean, punk, rap, and reggae. As the sleeve of a raï anthology shown in Figure 8 puts it:

Raï stars…love to state what time it is. Not that they like to waste words on religious or political issues—rising from the town of Oran in west Algerian in the '80s, raï was a celebration of good times in a place where good times were desperately hard to find. Sex 'n' drugs 'n' raï 'n' roll. Right on said Algeria's disaffected youth massive. Ruled out said Algeria's fundamentalist Islamic Front and military government, united in a hatred of raï's striving for freedom.

Here raï has been accommodated to the rigid protocols of Western youth culture—whose demands would not tolerate stories of raï's active promotion at times by the Algerian government, for example. In the versions produced for European record labels, moreover, the music itself has been adapted to suit Western tastes. In Khaled's songs, recorded with American musicians in Los Angeles for the 1992 album *Khaled* (the transition to the West was formally marked by his dropping the title *Cheb*), the distinctive and infinitely flexible three-beat rhythm of raï (triplets, in which the singer often freely extemporizes after the first beat) has been

8. Cover of raï compilation CD, Manteca World Music, 2000.

replaced by the mechanical fixed four-beat rhythm of Western
disco, with the addition of a recognizable Western-style
harmonized chorus. Khaled's voice, meanwhile, seems to refuse all
smoothed-out fusion, rasping out its Arabic on a separate track far
off in its own orbit, operating in another spatial rhythm and
temporality altogether. The commercial processes have also been
Westernized: whereas raï songs in Algeria were produced
spontaneously from a shifting range of communal sources, freely
adaptable by all, Khaled's record company have registered him
with the copyright authorities in France as the writer of all the
songs he had previously recorded in Algeria, even when they were
old songs of Cheikha Remitti and others that in Algeria had never
been regarded as anyone's private property. It was unlikely, of

course, that raï would ever have become popular in the West outside diasporic North African communities without some modifications, any more than Western music gets appropriated straight in the Maghreb. Moreover, as has been suggested, raï is itself a complex, changing musical form that remains adaptable and flexible: 'French' raï by Johanne Hayat or Malik is also popular in Algeria, while more Algerian singers increasingly sing only الراي النقي (pure raï)—with all its Islamic implications of propriety and avoidance of anything *haram*.

The CD cover picture in Figure 8 conveys important elements of raï rather better than its sleeve notes: its vibrancy and energy, its relations to masculinity, to the everyday experience of young Algerians on the streets, its continued active and positive relations to Islam, here signalled in the prominent prayer 'Bismillāh-ir-Rahmānir Rahīm' ('In the Name of Allah, the Gracious, the Merciful'), that closes and supports the whole image in the lower right corner. The montage thus gives something of a visual equivalent of raï's mixed social and religious identity.

Raï has often been described as 'hybrid'. Working in complex and sometimes covert ways by allusion and inference, raï has offered a creative space of articulation and demand, revolt and resistance, innovation and negotiation, for many of the contradictory social and economic channels operating within contemporary Algerian society: that's what a hybrid popular form can achieve. Raï encapsulates many of the creative characteristics generated out of irresolvable conflict, of intersectional experiences of change in societies violently fractured by colonial modernity—precisely the qualities that the term 'hybridity' in postcolonial writing seeks to locate.

Chapter 7
The ambivalence of the veil

Although the effects of migration and globalization mean that most cultures around the world are becoming increasingly hybridized, one very long-standing cultural and religious antithesis which goes back to the 7th century has returned to prominence in the 21st century: that between the Western and the Muslim worlds. And for many Westerners, nothing symbolizes the differences between them more clearly than the veil: they cannot stop talking about it, even while they legislate against it and its associated clothing—for example, banning the burkini on French beaches. As so often, it is women who are the target of attempts to control what they wear or do not wear. In the 19th century, the West considered the wearing of clothes as the mark of evolution and progress: it was 'savages' who went naked. Victorians modestly covered their bodies even when swimming. In the 20th and 21st centuries, however, near nudity and skimpy dress have become the signifier of the moral superiority of Western cultures.

Few items of clothing throughout history can have been given more meanings and political significances than 'the veil', a shorthand term for the variety of ways in which many Muslim women choose to dress, sometimes covering their heads or faces. For Europeans, the veil used to symbolize the erotic mysteries of the East, an association that remains widespread in popular culture. For Muslims, in the past it signified social status. Today, the meaning of the veil has changed dramatically. For Westerners the veil is often taken as a symbol of patriarchal Islamic societies in which women are assumed to be oppressed, subordinated, disempowered, and made invisible. Westerners forget that in earlier centuries, many women in Europe covered their hair in public with bonnets or coifs, or that, until comparatively recently, European Catholic women used to wear a mantle over their heads when going to church, just as orthodox Jews wear *kippahs* or *yarmulke*, *shtreimels*, and *sheitels* to fulfil the obligation to cover their heads. Today, in Islamic societies, and among many Muslim women in non-Islamic societies, the veil (*hijab*) has come to symbolize a cultural and religious identity, and women have increasingly chosen to cover themselves as a matter of choice. As a result, the veil is more widely worn today than ever before. Today, depending who you are, the veil symbolizes control or defiance, oppression or autonomy, patriarchy or non-Western communal values. How can we understand the veil, catch its meanings, and at the same time take hold of and interrogate our own automatic responses? No one can read the veil from a neutral, disinterested space. Let us try by first looking at an image (Figure 9) that typifies the kind of European stereotypical representations of the East in the colonial period, of the kind characterized by Edward Said as 'Orientalism'.

The image is entitled simply 'Arab woman'. A colour postcard, dating from around 1910, the high noon of imperialism, it was produced in Egypt by one of the many German photographic firms based in the Middle East at that time. The representation has objectified the woman it depicts. A real Egyptian woman, with a name, a family, a voice, and a history, has been transformed into an 'Oriental', a universal, generic, speechless 'Arab Woman'. The woman has been specially constructed for the eye of power suspended in the Westerner's gaze, and precipitated into the one-way street of 'the politics of recognition'.

9. 'Arab woman'.

She wears a brown veil, with a yellow lining that falls over her shoulders and a cloth of bluish-green. A *burqa* of black wrinkled cotton, held up by a *basma*, a piece of cloth that runs through the protruding *'oqla*, made from a piece of a special kind of bamboo called *Farsi*, covers the lower part of her face, but leaves much of her forehead and upper cheekbones exposed. She is looking away from the camera, thus increasing her modesty while at the same time giving her a thoughtful, distracted air. Looking at the coarse bluish cloth of her *galabiya* that falls in folds over the rest of her body, it seems that the artist has surreptitiously cast her in the pose of the Virgin Mary. A Virgin Mary, decently veiled, as indeed she is generally represented, and, it might seem, predominantly passive, receptive. All she lacks is the halo, but the aura of quietude around this woman is so strong that she hardly needs one.

With her averted gaze, and her arms lowered and folded around her body, it is as if she could never speak, or act, for herself.

Or is it we as viewers who assume this? Does this representation of a woman give us what the artist wanted us to see, a certain image of 'the Arab woman', an exotic oriental woman who can stand for all Arab women, as opposed to the reality of what this particular woman was really like? The image never asks us to think of her as a living human being in a social environment. It is constructed for a certain kind of Western viewer who already knows from many other representations what an 'Arab woman' ought to look like—modest, pining passively, above all veiled. The European knows her instantly, just as today people recognize a picture of a cosy snow-covered scene as an image of Christmas. Any representation of Christmas must show a snow-covered scene if it is going to evoke Christmas properly, even if in many, if not most, places of the world, Christmas actually never looks like that. In England, for example, it is generally a mild day with a bit of sunshine and drizzle. To show a drizzly day on a card, however, would not evoke 'Christmas' in the way a snow-scene does—even when we know that, in terms of our experience, it is almost never like that.

So too with this woman. Though her veiling here is not as extreme as in the full *burqa*, the tubular *'oqla* sticking out so prominently on the forehead, and the tightly drawn long black cloth round the cheekbones over the mouth, narrowing as it descends towards the waist like an enormous beak, give a strong impression to Western eyes of imprisonment. She seems literally confined, caged, exhibiting every quality that many Western women and men have considered that Muslim women need freeing from by the enlightened, unveiled West—the undressed West, which demands that women uncover themselves to show they are free, whether they want to or not.

The two layers of colour of the chromolithograph have not been swept over her eyes, leaving them almost matt, so that if you look closely at the pupils they are printed in black and white, staring out from behind the colours that veil her. You begin to see that her eyes are resourceful, strong, empowered, despite the aesthetic frame that has been put around her—which is far more repressive of what she really is than any veil could ever be. The stereotypical image becomes increasingly difficult to read. The woman who has been objectified seems to turn the tables and reassert herself against the power of the Western gaze.

In the course of the 20th century, the veil increasingly became a focus for those who sought to secularize Islamic societies. The French, in Algeria and elsewhere, initiated the 'Battle of the Veil', carrying out forced unveilings of local women. As part of his attempt to modernize Iran, the Western-imposed Shah of Iran banned the *chador*, the black head-to-toe body wrap worn by rural and traditional urban women. In direct response, after the Islamic Revolution of 1978/9, women were required to wear it. If some women can be considered to be persecuted by being forced to wear the veil, as Westerners generally assume, then other women are equally persecuted by secular laws that oblige them not to wear it. In France as in China, for example, girls are not allowed to go to school with their heads covered. An increasing number of countries have now taken steps to ban *burqas* and various forms of veiling. In Turkey, by contrast, the banning of the veil in public institutions that had existed since the time of secularist leader Kemal Atatürk (1881–1938) has recently been relaxed.

When people talk about 'the veil', they often end up talking about it as if it were a fixed thing, like a piece of uniform. There is not just 'the veil'—there are many kinds of veil, of covering, and in most societies at any given moment different women will be wearing a great variety of them, in untroubled heterogeneity. The veil itself is a fluid, ambivalent garment. There are the body veils, the *abaya*, the *burqa*, the *chador*, the *chadri*, the *carsaf* or *khimar*, the *haik*, and the *sitara*. Then there are the face or head veils, the *batula*, the *boushiya*, the *burko*, the *dupatta*, the *hijab*, the *niqaab*, the *rouband*, and the *yasmak*, to name only some of the most popular. While there are many different kinds of veil, and many distinct ways in which women wear any particular veil at specific times, like any clothing, veils also change, shift, modify, and are adapted to divergent needs and circumstances.

Such as colonial occupation, for example. Fanon emphasized what he called the 'historic dynamism of the veil', the ways in which it can be changed strategically and used instrumentally according to circumstance. This was particularly apparent during the Algerian War of Independence, when the division between the *colons* (settlers) and the natives was such that a woman affiliated herself to either side publicly according to her style of dress. As shown in the famous scenes in Pontecorvo's film *Battle of Algiers* (1965), Algerian women dressed as Europeans were sent as invisible couriers to carry weapons or plant bombs in the European parts of the city.

> The protective mantle of the Casbah, the almost organic curtain of
> safety that the Arab town weaves round the native, withdrew, and
> the Algerian woman, exposed, was sent forth into the conqueror's
> city. (Frantz Fanon)

By turns, Algeria veiled and unveiled itself, playing against the assumptions of the colonial occupier. Although the French soldiers were officially given leaflets telling them to respect Muslim women, there were many other well-documented occasions when the demands of their investigative processes, *la torture*, resulted in the rape, torture, and killing of suspects. Sometimes these women were paraded, bound and naked, by their captors, and photographed in that state before their death. Algeria unveiled—for the cruel eyes of French 'civilization'.

'This woman who sees without being seen frustrates the colonizer', says Fanon. She asserts a resisting refusal of knowledge comparable only to the impenetrability of the Casbah, the fortress in whose steep, narrow alleyways the veiled woman is often pictured. The Western response to the veil is to desire and demand its removal, so that contemporary strategies of liberation in the name of saving women supposedly forced to wear the veil coincide uncomfortably with the colonial violence of the veil's forcible removal.

Is it veiling or unveiling that constitutes the radical assertive move against institutionalized forms of power? Only recently, as it has become clear that many women choose to wear the veil and will fight for the right to do so, has veiling been associated with militancy amongst women. For men, by contrast, to wear the face veiled carries completely different connotations from those associated with the Arab woman. Take the photograph in Figure 10, for example, of Subcomandante Marcos of the Zapatistas riding triumphantly into Mexico City in 2001. Marcos has just criss-crossed the country in a fifteen-day march gathering support for his bill to increase rights of autonomy and land ownership for Mexico's still impoverished indigenous Indians. The government has finally agreed to negotiate with him, and Marcos rides into the city. It is a moment of popular frenzy. He is masked, garlanded, a popular hero.

To cover the face, for a man, carries all the connotations of wearing a mask—of romantic banditry, of being outlawed, adopting a disguise as a means of self-protection against the odds of the authority in power. The Zapatistas' war against the Mexican state on behalf of the indigenous peasantry of southern Mexico, who, despite rebellions throughout their history, have won few rights of land and property, has famously been one in which indigenous rights have been asserted through the most modern forms of technology as they come and go—fax, email, Facebook, Twitter, Instagram. At the same time, the Zapatistas have employed as their hallmark the balaclava helmet, a veil that, like the *keffiyeh* of the Palestinians, both guards their identity from the security forces and gives them a militant uniform. The very

10. Subcomandante Marcos arriving in Mexico City, 10 March 2001.

uniformity that the veil appears to impose on the woman here increases the masculine subversive resonance, just as with Batman's, the Lone Ranger's, or Zorro's masks. The male veil conjures up assertive resonances that are the very opposite of those projected onto veiled women. Whereas the Arab woman keeps demurely still, the garlanded Marcos raises his open hand triumphantly high in the air, and though he too looks to the side of the camera, he is clearly saluting a crowd, not averting his eyes from the viewer. We, as onlookers, are reduced to being part of the spectacle of which he is the centre. Why does the veil appear to disempower a woman, but empower a man?

The answer is that this is not intrinsically a gender issue but a situational one. There are also examples of veiling of Arab men, such as among the Amazigh Hamitic-speaking Tuareg, who regard the veil as an instrument of social status and masculinity. Tuareg men wear a white or blue veil called the *tegelmoust*. The Egyptian-born anthropologist Fadwa El Guindi writes,

> The veil is worn continually by men—at home, travelling, during the evening or day, eating or smoking, sleeping and even, according to some sources, during sexual intercourse.

Tuareg women, on the other hand, are not face-veiled at all, though they use their shawls to cover the lower part of the face rather as older women in South Asia use the *dupatta*. In the same way, Tuareg male veils are also used as a mobile signifier to denote meanings in everyday ordinary social intercourse. The veil is drawn up to the eyes before women, strangers, or prestigious persons, lowered amongst those for whom the wearer feels less respect. Rather as with the *dhoti* in southern India, which men unconsciously adjust, fold, wrap, and hitch up to knee length, then unfold and drop, as they stand talking to each other, Tuareg men are continually adjusting and readjusting their veils, heightening and tightening them, lowering and slackening, tugging and straightening them, as they go about their daily business.

The veil, in other words, can only be read in terms of its local meanings, which are generated within its own social space. A reading from outside will always tend to impose meanings from the assumptions of the viewer. For Westerners, the veil is about the subordination and oppression of women. In Arab societies, as El Guindi comments, 'the veil is about privacy, identity, kinship status, rank and class'. Whereas the Western viewer, therefore, typically sees the photograph of the veiled Arab woman as a symbol of women's oppression under Islam, for an Egyptian looking at her image in 1910, the veil would have symbolized the woman's social rank. Women of the lowest class, particularly the peasantry in the countryside and the Bedouin women of the desert, would not have worn a veil at all. Within the cities, women of different classes wore different kinds of veil. Upper-class Egyptian women wore the Turkish-style *bisha*, made of white muslin. The woman in the postcard, by contrast, wears a traditional black face-veil and *'oqla*, which, together with her *galabiya*, suggests that she belongs to the lower classes of artisans, labourers, or market women. While to the Western viewer, therefore, her image may suggest either biblical resonances or an oppressive patriarchal social system, to an Egyptian, her veil first and foremost would have defined her social status. The Western viewer, in other words, with no local cultural knowledge, would give a completely different interpretation of the photograph to that of the contemporary Egyptian woman whom it represented.

Nowadays the veil involves a different kind of cultural power, particularly with respect to Western societies. Take Figure 11, for example, in which the veiled black woman clearly communicates her challenge directly to the spectator. Her eyes are wide open, and she looks straight at the camera. Notice, too, how the image is taken close up, in an in-your-face way, rather than inviting the aesthetic distance through which we saw the Arab woman. Our response is mediated by the information provided by the caption, which tells us that she is a Muslim woman photographed in Brooklyn, New York. The fact that she is in New York encourages

11. 'Muslim woman in Brooklyn' by Chester Higgins Jr.

the viewer to assume that she is an African-American woman who is probably a member of the Nation of Islam. She has chosen the veil, in the society in which it currently has the most confrontational meaning.

Veil, mask: compliance or defiance? And agency: who chooses to veil themselves? In fact, the women's and the Zapatistas' choice of veiling are responses to the society in which they live. It might seem that the Egyptian woman has no option within a patriarchal system but to veil herself, while Marcos has been a free agent who makes a choice. However, as we have seen, in fact in Egypt in the earlier part of the 20th century, veiling for a woman was generally a mark of status, and was therefore regarded as empowering rather than disempowering. One reason veiling became more widespread was because more and more women wanted to assert social status, particularly to other women. Today it may have other meanings or functions. In countries where sexual harassment by men is widespread, particularly for example when travelling on buses to work, wearing the *hijab* can also function as a form of self-protection. Add a pair of large dark glasses, and you are also nicely protected from surveillance cameras. For men a hoodie conveniently serves the same function. But who interprets a hoodie in terms of oppression and lack of freedom? Covering the face has become a widespread means of avoiding identification by police cameras, a device always used, for example, at IRA funerals, and by demonstrators around the world who wish to avoid facial recognition cameras. Wearing the Anonymous Guy Fawkes mask also represents an act of defiance and assertion, as veiling does for some Islamic women today.

In 2020 people all around the world suddenly became aware of the practical utility of veiling when they began to wear facemasks to protect themselves against the Corona virus. The meaning of the veil, when it has one, is never stable. Fanon recalls how under colonial rule Moroccan women changed the colour of their veil from white to black to express solidarity with their exiled king: they chose to give the veil a meaning by transforming its colour. To wear any form of the veil is always a performance that signifies something. To interpret that meaning, especially in Western countries, by reading it out of its own social context and imposing another perspective on it, has very little to do with what the veil means for the actual woman who is wearing it.

Chapter 8
Gender, queering, and feminism in a postcolonial context

Just as the meaning of the veil shifts from period to period, so too do other attributes associated with gender, to the extent that in the 21st century the very idea of gender, particularly the idea that it comprises just two forms, 'male' and 'female', has been challenged, queered, and unravelled.

Until the 1970s or 1980s, if you used the word 'gender' in English you would generally be referring to the grammatical categories he/she/it. The use of the word 'gender' to mean the cultural rather than biological characteristics of femininity and masculinity, and the ways in which people represent themselves in terms of their social gender role, was first used in English in 1955, but only came into popular use after the 1970s. There are many languages in which the concept of gender, which distinguishes between biological sex and gender as the performance of a social role, still lacks an exact equivalent term (the same is true for associated words such as 'empowerment'). In the same period, in Western countries there was a shift in attitude towards gender identities that do not conform to the conventional masculine/feminine binary. Many states decriminalized homosexuality, while activists reinscribed associated words in English such as 'gay' and 'queer' as positive terms. More recently, 'queer' and 'queering' have been adopted more widely to describe a strategy of shifting social or intellectual perspectives out of their dominant binary forms—in that sense, a postcolonial perspective is one that almost by definition queers its objects of study. Sexual orientations that had previously been medicalized as illnesses, 'perversions', or psychiatric disorders were normalized and became socially acceptable, with the exception of paedophilia and pederasty, which conversely were stigmatized more than ever.

For some time, the gender binary was challenged in favour of including a third gender, examples of which can be found in many cultures around the world, such as the *hijras* in South Asia. Now, however, gender has come to be seen as more of a continuum rather than an opposition, or a specific number, with a spectrum of non-binary gender identities acknowledged in the acronym LGBTQ+, which designates shifting varieties of sexualities and genders. Politically, LGBTQ+ is considered to have minority status by analogy with ethnic and linguistic minorities. All these transformations for the most part originated in the European, North American, and Australasian academies where gender and sexuality became objects of study in their own right. At the same time, they were articulated as forms of identity politics: again by analogy with ethnicity, your sexuality could become your primary form of identity.

In the Global South, responses to these developments were varied. There were many countries in which laws against homosexuality still existed, though these were often the legacy of colonial rule which had prescribed the norms of sexual behaviour for colonies according to the then current European ideas. Colonial rule enforced European 19th-century sexual mores on societies where gender roles and practices of sexuality were often more fluid and less restricted—indeed that was the attraction for some Europeans who went out to the colonies. Today, it is often in societies of the South where patriarchal norms, or hypermasculine role models, are strongest, that the greatest resistance can be found to more flexible ideas of gender, which are sometimes portrayed as yet another instance of Western cultural imperialism. Queering the norms of such cultures, in Africa, the Middle East, or the Caribbean for example, has become a major, sometimes controversial, arena of postcolonial gender politics. The question, often implicitly an objection, raised here is how universal are contemporary Western ideas about gender? What are the cultural politics of LGBTQ+ activism in other cultures?

These differences also work in reverse. While most in the West are now more open and less judgemental with respect to different forms and practices of sexuality, many still find it hard to accept conventions and forms of behaviour where they appear to be more restrictive, especially with respect to the social mores and customs of Islamic societies regarding women. Western attitudes can be accused of falling into the traditional colonial position that Gayatri Spivak has characterized as 'white men saving brown women from brown men'. Today the difference would be that it is white women who try to save brown women.

Does feminism have to mean 'Westernization'? Mainstream feminist activism in the countries of the South goes back at least to the 19th century. The same arguments were heard then. Things were complicated by the fact that for some women under colonial rule, particularly those from the middle classes, European women provided role models of independence and agency. Some colonized women spoke of a 'double colonization'—first that of the colonial power, and then that of patriarchy.

Another way of thinking about these issues can be by resituating them in terms of the politics of modernity. Many characteristics of modernity were, in fact, the invention of women. Modernity is defined both by its technology and its political concepts of equality and democracy, which necessarily involve the end of patriarchy and the institution of equal rights for women (as well as for minorities and other subaltern groups). For many male nationalists, on the other hand, modernity was a matter of reorienting the economy, the state, the public sphere. Even today, as the Indian novelist Arundhati Roy has acerbically pointed out, the Hindutva quest for authentic Indianness according to a carefully constructed fantasy of the past would not go so far as dispensing with the mobile phone, the railways, aeroplanes, or rockets that deliver atomic bombs. Gandhi was in fact much more radical than modern Hindutva ideologues in extending his critique of Western civilization to science and technology, rejecting the railways and other aspects of colonial modernity in his book *Hind Swaraj* (*Indian Home Rule*; 1909) Some of the ideas that he put forward there were the forerunner of contemporary notions of 'sustainable development', the art of the possible that will not destroy the planet.

When nationalism moved from reform movements to cultural revival, feminists began to part company from it, while continuing to appropriate elements of modernity for their own political goals. Cultural nationalists tended to define themselves not against modernity in terms of technology, but against its implications for women. As we've seen, women are often taken to represent the mainstay of the cultural identity of the nation, retrieved for the present from the society of the past. For macho-nationalists, home and the domestic sphere, relatively free from colonial control, was the best guardian of the traditional values, culture, and identity of the new phenomenon of 'the nation' that they were creating on the European model against their European masters. Women and modernity came to be regarded as antithetical entities, with the result that the goal of national emancipation involved a betrayal of all prospect of progressive change for women. This was spectacularly dramatized in India and Africa on the occasions when the colonial government attempted to outlaw practices such as child marriage, widow-burning, and female genital mutilation. The preservation of these practices became celebrated causes for male nationalist resistance.

Such interventions by the colonial state against social practices that oppressed women have been described as 'colonial feminism', that is where the colonial government intervened on behalf of women, claiming it was doing so on humanitarian grounds. As with today's practice of 'humanitarian intervention', sometimes such measures operated simultaneously as forms of colonial control. The colonial authorities were often sympathetic to those interventions that they regarded as a way of transforming the values of societies whose traditions resisted their rule, and here women were regarded as a key component in any challenge to tradition. It was entirely predictable that such legislative acts would become the focus for nationalist opposition. Yet paradoxically, for women colonial ideology could also represent new forms of freedom. As a result, women were much more ambivalently placed in relation to both colonialism and anti-colonial nationalism.

In the same way, when women struggle with patriarchal social structures in the postcolonial era, they are repeatedly accused of importing Western ideas. Well-meaning interventions by Western feminists, human rights groups, and global North-funded non-governmental organizations can at times end up by making life more complicated for local feminists. Development of all kinds works best from below rather than being imposed from above or outside.

At the same time, if you argue that feminism is a Western idea then you would have to claim that modernity itself is exclusively Western. Historically, it is true that feminism was a Western political movement that began in the 18th century, its beginnings indistinguishable from those of modernity itself. Modernity, however, was less of a Western invention than a product of the West's interaction with the rest of the world, including the economic exploitation of colonialism and the development of the colonies as markets for industrial goods which provided the surplus that was one motor for modern capitalism. Since then modernity has developed in different ways and according to different temporalities in different places, and the same is true of feminism. Like other aspects of modernity, its progress over the past two centuries within non-Western worlds has transformed and nuanced its precepts. All political programmes of today, whether feminist or those seeking to recreate ancient national glories, are products of their own age and therefore very much part of modernity. The same is true for all forms of religious fundamentalism—even if the ideological message is that of a return to a 'purer' past, which was a foundational conceit of Protestantism and Romanticism. The debate is not between modernity and its opponents, but rather between different versions of modernity, some of which offer alternatives to what is regarded, not always very accurately, as the Western model.

Women's movements after independence

Many of these differences remained relatively suppressed while men and women worked together for the common aims of the anti-colonial movements. It was after independence that fundamental tensions emerged more clearly. 'The Role of Women Does Not End with Peace' was the simple but astute title of an article by the Egyptian feminist Amina al-Sa'id about Egyptian women volunteering for the army in 1956 (Figure 12). For all feminists, the transfer of power at independence and the achievement of national sovereignty, though desirable, was not the end. It was simply a stage along the way. Whereas from a masculine perspective, independence ushered in the new state of postcoloniality, for women there was no such break: the struggle continued, now against a patriarchal sphere that no longer required women's support. Independence very often involved a transfer of power not to 'the people' of the newly sovereign country, but to local elites who inherited the whole colonial system of the army, the police, the judiciary and the law, government bureaucracy, education, and development agencies. In many states, with the achievement of national sovereignty women's political objectives had to be reasserted and a second liberation struggle begun. For this reason, postcolonial politics has often

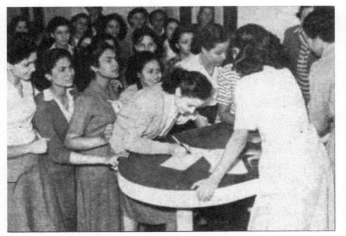

12. Egyptian women volunteer for popular resistance movements against British occupation.

more in common with women's than men's struggles of the colonial era, with a politics of egalitarianism that supports diversity.

The development of religious nationalisms such as Hindutva, or Islamic fundamentalisms, in political forms and the decline of socialism as an ideal in the postcolonial era has actually placed some women in a situation comparable to that in which they found themselves during colonialism. Women in Islamic countries, however, are not simply oppressed by fundamentalism or by Islam, as liberals in the West often assume. There is no single Islam, nor a single Islamic fundamentalism. Women in Islamic countries are positioned in relation to the specificities of their own cultures, their own histories, their own relations to the West, their own struggles over the interpretation of Islam and of Islamic law, and the role of women in contemporary society.

Conversely, contrary to the polemics that can sometimes be heard, there is no single undifferentiated 'West' either. The West is just as fractured and diverse as everywhere else, politically and even economically.

What makes postcolonial feminism 'postcolonial'?

Can postcolonial feminism be distinguished from other categories such as 'third-world feminism' or 'women in third-world politics'? At its most general, postcolonial feminism involves any challenge to dominant patriarchal ideologies by women of the third world. Such political activism may consist of contesting local power structures, or it may be a question of challenging racist or Eurocentric views of men and women (including feminists) in the first world. Postcolonial feminism begins from the perception that its politics are framed by the active legacies of colonialism, by the institutional infrastructures that were handed over by the colonial powers to elite, typically male groups, or appropriated by later elites. All women working for equality against the many obstacles embedded in such a framework engage with these kinds of realities in the postcolony. Women's struggles make clearest the fact that while the anti-colonial campaigns were directed against the colonial regime towards the political goal of sovereignty, postcolonial struggles are directed against the postcolonial state as well as against the Western interests that may enforce its neo-colonial status. In much academic writing about postcolonialism, more emphasis has been placed on historical analysis of the processes of combating colonialism than on the political philosophy of the movements that challenge contemporary forms of power in the postcolonial state. With feminists, it has been the other way around.

The general use of the term 'postcolonial' to mean, literally, in a historical sense, 'after the colonial' may be applied to a whole range of different politics. Any political act in a postcolonial state may by definition technically be able to claim the term postcolonial, but this does not mean that such acts involve the politics of the postcolonial, any more than mass political movements in which many women are involved necessarily incorporate gender perspectives. Even those women whose activities can properly be described as postcolonial from a situational and ideological point of view cannot be characterized as operating according to the same paradigm. Take the difference, for example, between the work of two prominent Tunisian lawyers, Radhia Nasraoui and Gisèle Halimi. Nasraoui lives in Tunisia and is well-known there for fighting the human rights abuses of the postcolonial Tunisian state, without any specific feminist agenda, particularly during the rule of the authoritarian President Zine El Abidine Ben Ali, who was deposed at the beginning of the Arab Spring in January 2011. Halimi moved from Tunisia to France, trained as a lawyer, and came to prominence with her legal campaign on behalf of Djamila Boupacha, a young Algerian girl tortured by the police in French Algeria in 1961. Since this *cause célèbre*, which brought her the friendship of Simone de Beauvoir and of Jean-Paul Sartre, Halimi has defended Basque terrorists in court, and also worked as a lawyer on issues relating to women, particularly the Bobigny abortion trial of 1972. In 1971, she founded the group *Choisir*, which was formed to defend women who deliberately made public the fact that they had had illegal abortions. *Choisir*'s ensuing campaign was a major factor in the decision by the French government to make abortion legal in France in 1974. Halimi went on to become a Deputy in the French National Assembly and a French delegate to UNESCO. She returned to wider public prominence in October 2000 as one of the signatories of the manifesto demanding that the French people admit and face up to the history of the systematic use of torture by the French colonial authorities against the Algerian people, and calling for the condemnation of such practices in a public statement by the President and Prime Minister. Halimi has been one of the major instigators of the memory work of forcing France to confront the postcolonial legacies of its colonial history. This has initiated a profound rethinking, reworking, and re-estimation of the ethics of the ruthless French campaign to suppress Algerian independence, the traumatic effects of which continue to reverberate in both countries.

What makes a politics postcolonial?

The work of both women can be described as postcolonial, but as women activists their politics remain distinct. The specific conditions for women in postcolonial states, or the postcolonial conditions in metropolitan states for women migrants, will always vary according to location, which means that there cannot be a single form of postcolonial politics. What makes a politics postcolonial is a broader shared political philosophy that guides its ethics and its practical aims. Postcolonialism as a political philosophy means first and foremost the right to autonomous self-government of those who still find themselves in a situation of being controlled politically and administratively by a foreign or external power. With sovereignty achieved, a postcolonial politics will seek to change the basis of the state itself, actively transforming the restrictive, centralizing hegemony of the cultural nationalism that may have been required for the struggle against colonialism. It stands for empowering the poor, the dispossessed, and the disadvantaged, for tolerance of difference and diversity, for the establishment of minorities' rights, women's rights, LGBTQ+ rights, and cultural rights within a broad framework of democratic egalitarianism that refuses to impose alienating Western ways of thinking on tricontinental societies. It resists all forms of exploitation (environmental as well as human), racism, and all oppressive conditions that have been developed solely for the interests of corporate capitalism. It challenges the commodification of social relations and the doctrine of individualism that functions as the means through which such interests are achieved. It resists all exploitation that results from comparative poverty or powerlessness—from the appropriation of natural resources, to unjust prices for commodities and crops, to the international sex trade. A postcolonial politics stands for the right to basic amenities—security, sanitation, health care, food, and education—for all peoples of the earth, young, adult, and elderly; women, men, and non-binary people. It champions the cause not only of industrial workers but also those underclasses, those groups marginalized according to gender, ethnicity, or simply the kind of labour that they perform, that have not hitherto been considered to qualify for radical class politics. While encouraging personal ethics of sincerity and altruism, it questions attempts to return to national or cultural 'authenticity', which it regards as largely constructed for dubious political purposes. It considers most productive those forms of intersectional thought that interact freely across disciplines and cultures in constructive dialogues that undo the hierarchies of power.

Postcolonialism, with its fundamental sympathies for the subaltern, for the peasantry, for the poor, for outcasts of all kinds, eschews the high culture of the elite and espouses subaltern cultures and knowledges which have historically been considered of little value but which it regards as rich repositories of culture and counter-knowledge. Postcolonial sympathies and interests are focused on those at the margins of society, those whose cultural identity has been dislocated or left uncertain by the forces of global capitalism—refugees, migrants who have moved from the countryside to the impoverished edges of the city, migrants who struggle in the first world for a better life while working at the lowest levels of those societies. At all times, postcolonialism stands for a transformational politics, for a decolonial politics dedicated to the removal of inequality—from the different degrees of wealth of the different states in the uneven world system of nations, to the class, ethnic, and other social hierarchies within individual states, to the racialized and gendered hierarchies that operate at every level of social and cultural relations. Postcolonialism combines and draws on elements from radical socialism, feminism, and environmentalism. Its difference from any of these as generally defined is that it begins from a fundamentally tricontinental, third-world, subaltern perspective while its priorities always focus on the Global South. In short, the postcolonial looks at, experiences, and values the world from below rather than from above.

The framework of postcolonial politics is such that gender constitutes one of its enabling conditions. The inseparable centrality of gender politics to postcolonial politics can be simply illustrated by contrasting it to the phrase 'women in third-world politics', the title of a chapter in a widely used textbook on comparative third-world politics. The masculist assumption here is that there is a ready-made constituency—third-world politics—and that women can be adequately catered for by analysing how they operate within it. Politics by implication is a fundamentally masculine social space: the chapter will look at how women operate within a world that is not of their making. A postcolonial perspective, on the other hand, starts from the premise that there is no third-world politics without women, and that women have broadly defined much of what constitutes the political. Women therefore not only operate as political activists, but also have typically constituted the political arena in which they work. One of the distinctive aspects of feminist activism is that generally it is always situated in relation to particular social and institutional practices, whether it be education, law, or medicine and its relation to the body. It can also combine powerfully with other contemporary political concerns, for example ecology, where women have often led the way.

Whereas traditional Marxist analyses had always emphasized the role of women factory workers, Western feminists argued from the 1960s onwards for the political significance of women's domestic work, and of the domestic sphere in general. This was then subsumed by greater emphasis on subjectivity and sexuality, with recourse to psychoanalysis and issues of identity. Postcolonial feminism is certainly concerned to analyse the nervous conditions of being a woman in a postcolonial environment, whether in the social oppression of the postcolony or the metropolis. Its concern is not in the first place with individual problems but with those that affect whole communities. For this reason, it places greater emphasis on social and political campaigns for material, cultural, and legal rights; equal treatment in the law, education, and the workplace; the environment; and the differences between the values that feminists outside the West may encounter and those that they may wish to support. As activism, it involves grassroots campaigns rather than party politics. Not that a postcolonial politics eschews political intervention in the traditional space of the political, though it does not stop at a national level, as such political spaces customarily do. Postcolonial politics is fundamentally, in conception and practice, a transnational politics, operating from below across the continents through alliances of ordinary people working together.

Postcolonial feminism has never operated as a discrete or separate entity, for it has directly inspired the forms and the force of postcolonial politics. Where its feminist focus is foregrounded, it comprises non-Western feminisms which negotiate the political demands of nationalism, populism, socialist-feminism, liberalism, and ecofeminism, alongside the social challenge of everyday patriarchy, typically supported by its institutional and legal discrimination: of domestic violence, sexual abuse, rape, honour killings, dowry deaths, female foeticide, child abuse. Feminism in a postcolonial frame begins with the situation of the ordinary woman in a particular place, while also thinking her situation through in relation to broader issues to give her the more powerful basis of collectivity. It will highlight the degree to which women are still working against a colonial legacy that was itself powerfully patriarchal—institutional, economic, political, and ideological.

Typically, writing about tricontinental women's political activism profiles movements and organizations, rather than parties or individuals, or analyses the oppression of particular groups, for example migrant women workers, sweatshop workers, or sex workers. This is common to writing about other subaltern forms of resistance, peasant movements, or anti-capitalist organizations.

In a comparable way, only rarely do subalterns who espouse active forms of postcolonial politics achieve access to mainstream forms of political power, as did the Brazilian Luiz Inácio da Silva (Lula) of the Workers' Party when he was elected President of Brazil in August 2002.

13. Phoolan Devi, with her gang, on her way to the surrender ceremony at the village of Bhind, India, 12 February 1983 (*Yagdish Yadar*).

A good example of a subaltern woman activist who achieved political power was Phoolan Devi, the low-caste *dasyu sundari* ('beautiful bandit'), as she was called by local people in the Chambal region of India where she operated as the undisputed queen of the ravines. Devi became notorious after the massacre of twenty upper-caste *thakurs* (landowners) at Behmai in Uttar Pradesh in 1981, carried out in revenge for a *thakur*'s gang rape perpetrated on her (the worst of many abuses she had suffered). After her dramatic surrender in 1983 (Figure 13), with which she renounced her own embittered violence and rough justice, she spent many years in jail. Eventually, however, she became a member of parliament, announcing her desire to work for the poor, the downtrodden, the exploited, and the so-called 'most backward castes'. This indeed is what she proceeded to do, though far more media space has been taken up discussing the merits, or lapses, of the film about her early life, *Bandit Queen*, than has ever been devoted to her political work. Phoolan was a dramatic and highly visible symbol of the political assertion of subaltern women and the oppressed lower castes of India. Her very presence effected a continuing protest against the deeply entrenched, oppressive treatment of Dalits in India. Phoolan Devi was herself assassinated in July 2001. As popular hero, she became the first woman to join the symbolic iconography of champions of the poor and oppressed, alongside Che Guevara, Frantz Fanon, and Subcomandante Marcos.

Chapter 9
Globalization from a postcolonial perspective

Che reads *The Wretched of the Earth*

March 1965: an Air Cubana Bristol Britannia turbo-prop aircraft flying from Prague to Havana develops engine trouble and makes an unscheduled stop at Shannon airport in the west of Ireland, and the passengers are forced to camp out there for a couple of days. One night, having run out of cigars, they go into Limerick to try to see a cowboy film, but can't find one. So instead, they drop into a local pub, Hanratty's Hotel, and order some beers. In the jostle of the packed bar, a local Irishman bumps into one of the Cubans and slops his beer all over his bearded companion. It was Che Guevara.

The wet but warm Irish welcome produced a few characteristic wisecracks from Che, whose great-grandfather Patrick Lynch had emigrated from Mayo in the west of Ireland in the 18th century. In time-honoured local style, Che cheerfully just ordered another beer. Che spent much of his time talking to one of the other Cubans, the great poet and critic Roberto Fernández Retamar, then Director of the famous Cuban publishing house Casa de las Americas. Che recommended to Retamar that he have a book translated for Cuban publication that had increasingly preoccupied him on the tour of Africa from which he was returning. The book was Frantz Fanon's *The Wretched of the*

Earth, published in Paris—and almost immediately impounded by the French police—just four years before.

Revolutionary Africa had infiltrated revolutionary South America, except of course that if revolutionary Africa was represented by Fanon, he had come from the Caribbean in the first place. You could say that there have been not one but three revolutionary Africas in the 20th century: the revolutionary Africa of the Maghreb, notably the Algerian War of Independence (1954–62); the revolutionary sub-Saharan Africa whose insurrectional impulses were encouraged by Fanon and directly aided by Guevara in his Congo campaign; and finally the revolutionary Africa from which Fanon originally came—the revolutionary, African-American tradition of the USA which was historically always inextricably mixed with Caribbean radicalism. The famous Che-Lumumba Club, the militant all-black collective of the Communist Party in Los Angeles in the 1960s, was one iconic manifestation of that revolutionary African-Caribbean impulse, as was the revival of a black socialism, self-consciously affiliated to Cuban tricontinental revolutionary struggle, by Stokely Carmichael, Leroi Jones, and Huey P. Newton, leader of the Black Panthers. What's noticeable here is that half of the name of that militant all-black collective should have been that of a white man: Che. But, after all, as a Latino in the United States, Che was not quite white.

Che's writings and speeches show a marked change in this period—as his focus shifts from building socialism in Cuba to a Fanonian vision of a world split between exploitative imperialist and progressive socialist countries. The murder of Patrice Lumumba, the remarkable President of the newly liberated Congo, as a part of 'Project Wizard', a CIA 'covert action program' which took place under the condoning eye of the United Nations, together with the war being waged by the United States against the Vietnamese, gave a new sense that formal independence was only the beginning of a new era of a different kind of domination by the West. Fanon's powerful *The Wretched of the Earth* was the inspiration of that anti-imperialist moment. The book's most difficult aspect comes with Fanon's argument for the use of violence in anti-colonial struggle. He justified this on the grounds that violence, not civilization or the rule of law, was the constitutive condition of colonialism itself. Colonial rule, he maintained, was merely an attempt to legitimate and normalize the acts of colonial violence by which the colony had been occupied in the first place and by which colonial rule was subsequently maintained.

After its publication in 1961, *The Wretched of the Earth* very rapidly became the bible of decolonization, inspiring many different kinds of struggle against domination and oppression across the world. When the first English translation of *Les Damnés de la terre* was published by Présence Africaine in Paris in 1963, it was called simply *The Damned*. Two years later, when it was published in London, it was renamed and given the title by which it is now known, *The Wretched of the Earth*. The following year it was published in the United States, with an additional subtitle: *A Negro Psychoanalyst's Study of the Problems of Racism & Colonialism in the World Today*. By the time the book was reissued in 1968 as an African-American mass-market paperback, the subtitle had changed. Now it was *The Handbook for the Black Revolution that is Changing the Shape of the World*. Think of the reversal of agency that the book itself achieved in five years: from *The Damned* to *The Handbook for the Black Revolution that is Changing the Shape of the World*.

Fanon's tendency to identify and analyse oppression and injustice in its many forms universally rather than locally, his powerfully expressed humanism, his emphasis on the revolutionary primacy of the peasantry, align him quite closely with Che—another famous internationalist revolutionary and committed activist, another *déraciné* man of routes, who was almost his exact contemporary and who died similarly young (their respective dates are 1925–61, 1928–67). In December 1964, Guevara had delivered his devastating denunciation of imperialism to the United Nations in New York. It was during this visit that Che was invited up to Harlem by Malcolm X, like Castro before him, but felt unable to go given that the US government was already incensed by his UN speech—Che judged that to speak in Harlem would be interpreted as an intervention in US internal affairs. So instead he sent a message of solidarity, which Malcolm X read out, adding:

> This is from Che Guevara. I'm happy to hear your warm round of applause in return because it lets the white man know that he's not just in a position to tell us who we should applaud for and who we shouldn't applaud for. And you don't see any anti-Castro Cubans around here—we eat them up.

True to this African solidarity, after his United Nations appearance, Guevara flew to Africa and embarked on a punishing round of conferences and diplomatic missions in Africa and the Middle East similar to those on which Fanon had travelled four years before—except that Guevara also followed the footsteps of the black Pan-Africanist W. E. B. Du Bois and threw in a visit to China for good measure. It was during this trip around Africa that Guevara first read and lived the realities of *The Wretched of the Earth*. On a visit to Algiers in 1965, he was interviewed by Josie Fanon, Fanon's widow, for *Révolution Africaine*, and spoke to her of the importance of Africa as a field of struggle against imperialism, colonialism, and neo-colonialism. In homage to Fanon's humanism, Guevara also wrote his greatest essay during this trip, 'Socialism and Man in Cuba' (1965), an eloquent, passionate argument for a society based on human values, that could only begin by changing consciousness itself. For Che, what he characterized as the new man and the new woman were inexorably part of the development of a new society. Socialism, he argued, cannot be imposed from above: it must be produced as an ethical as well as material commitment from the people themselves.

In his final, dispiriting expedition to Bolivia, contrary to his expectations, Che did not succeed in eliciting support and solidarity for his revolutionary politics from the local indigenous peoples in the only country in Latin America where they constitute a majority of the population. After his execution by the Bolivian army, Guevara became the icon of social revolution: both men have become far more famous, as dynamic legends, after their deaths. *Che vive.*

Like Che, one of Fanon's greatest qualities was his charismatic ability to inspire others. The latter's publisher, François Maspero, described the basis of Fanon's contemporary appeal in performative terms that could equally apply to Che.

> Numerous were those, who, like myself, discovered in [Fanon's] *Towards the African Revolution* the basis of their commitment and the answer to 'why we are fighting', which, hitherto, had been so cruelly lacking. We saw in Fanon's appeal only an appeal to fraternity.

A similar response was given by Fanon's first publisher and editor, the radical activist Francis Jeanson, who in his preface to the original edition of *Black Skin, White Masks* (1952) wrote:

> The Revolt might, perhaps, never attain its end but its only chance of doing so resides in those men who are too impatient to accommodate themselves to the rhythm of History, too demanding to admit that they have nothing else to do in this world—which by chance is also theirs—but to prepare, in the resignation of their own failure, the triumph of a distant humanity.

The intellectual background of the two men was remarkably similar, a heady mixture of Sartre, existential philosophy, psychoanalysis, Marx, and Mao. Both were men of great physical as well as intellectual intensity. Fanon's emphasis on violence at times seems to describe nothing less than his own excessive ardour, his force, stress, fury, and impatience, as well as the physicality of language and manner that was so distinctive a feature of his writing and personality. His description of the radical Cameroonian leader Félix Moumié (known as the Ho Chi Minh of the Cameroons) sounds like no other than Fanon himself:

> the most concrete, the most alive, the most impetuous man. Félix's tone was constantly high. Aggressive, violent, full of anger, in love with his country, hating cowards and maneuverers. Austere, hard, incorruptible. A bundle of revolutionary spirit packed into 60 kilos of muscle and bone.

Finally, Fanon and Guevara shared a further bond: neither were professional revolutionaries, nor even professional politicians— rather they were both middle-class professionals who became revolutionaries as a result of a conviction that the conditions which they treated were the product of social, rather than physical or individual, ills. Their humane tricontinental socialism came out of the realities of their own lived experience and their compassion for and sympathy with the oppressed.

In this connection it is important to recall that in fact, remarkably, both Fanon and Guevara were trained doctors, who continued to practise their healing skills right to the end, even as they simultaneously carried on their day-to-day commitments to violent revolution. This apparent paradox, an ethics of healing through revolutionary violence, remains at the heart of the lives and works of both Guevara and Fanon. They thought of this by analogy with the practices of medicine itself: to cure the open wound of colonial rule by surgical intervention rather than the earlier Gandhian strategy of a therapeutic homeopathy. The challenging ethics of their politics was best described by the Martiniquan poet and politician Aimé Césaire in his powerful posthumous tribute to Fanon:

> If the word 'commitment' has any meaning, it was with Fanon that it acquired significance. A violent one, they said. And it is true that

Fanon instituted himself as a theorist of violence, the only arm of the colonised that can be used against colonialist barbarity.

But his violence, and this is not paradoxical, was that of the nonviolent. By this I mean the violence of justice, of purity and intransigence. This must be understood about him: his revolt was ethical and his endeavour generous.

His revolt was ethical and his endeavour generous. Like Guevara's, Fanon's revolt was also one of indomitable will: 'Socialismo o muerte!'

Globalization

The postcolonial world is a place of uneven mixture. Since the Canadian philosopher Marshall McLuhan invented the concept of the global village in 1968, the cultures of the world have become increasingly interlayered, combined, and juxtaposed. Largely a product of technology, of instantaneous media systems by means of which anything that happens in the world can instantly be seen everywhere else, the inexorable forces of globalization have increasingly brought the world's economies into a single system, particularly after the fall of the Soviet Union and the so-called Eastern Bloc in the early 1990s. While multi- and transnational companies looked to global markets for growth now impossible to achieve in the mature markets of the West, they simultaneously lowered their cost base by outsourcing manufacturing or administration to any country that was poor and reasonably politically stable (a strict authoritarian regime like China will do nicely). There are few societies today that have not felt the impact of their place, whatever it is, in the world economy and the international division of labour.

At one level, this means certain aspects of the world, particularly the production of commodities, are being standardized, so that everyone buys the same products wherever they may be—from toothpaste to cars, from world literature to globalized university degrees. Yet the impact of multi- or transnationals goes two ways. It is easier to put pressure on such companies to end practices of exploitation or environmental degradation than it is with local maverick firms that may not be amenable to complaints from far away, such as the logging or mining companies in the Amazon. By contrast, companies such as Shell or Nike have eventually proved themselves susceptible to international pressure with regard to their local practices. Shell notoriously allowed its Nigerian subsidiary to continue for years in a whole range of activities that contributed to the oppression of the Ogoni people and degraded the local environment. After sustained campaigning by activists (led by the Nigerian novelist Ken Saro-Wiwa until his execution), it eventually changed its ways.

'Good food—Nestlé—Good life'

Some multinationals continue to court bad publicity. Nestlé, the Swiss corporation that has grown into the biggest food company in the world, has a history of doing so. In December 2002 the company announced that it was pursuing a legal action for $6 million compensation from the Ethiopian government for a business that the previous government nationalized in 1975, but whose rights Nestlé itself only acquired in 1986 when it bought the firm's parent German company. The government of Ethiopia, one of the poorest nations on earth, at that time suffering from its worst famine in twenty years with six million people who required emergency food aid, had offered $1.5 million. Nestlé, however, was seeking full compensation, at 1975 exchange rates. The effects of the famine had been intensified by the collapse of international coffee prices: coffee supports a quarter of the Ethiopian population. At that time, Ethiopia had the lowest income per person in the world, around $100 a year, and more than one-tenth of its children died before their first birthday. Nestlé, the world's largest coffee producer, made an annual profit of $5.5 billion in

2001. An average Ethiopian yearly income would then buy just 50 grams of Nescafé a week from 'the world's leading food company'.

The news of Nestlé's action produced front-page headlines, coverage on radio and TV news, and such an avalanche of emailed global protest that the company quickly changed its position. On 19 December the Nestlé spokesperson had said the company had to take the Ethiopian government to court for its $6 million as a 'matter of principle'. By the very next day, the company offered to reinvest in Ethiopia all the proceeds that it received from the legal claim. The London *Financial Times* put it bluntly:

> The Swiss company, one of the world's richest and most powerful, made the offer yesterday in a bid to reduce a damaging public outcry over its long-running compensation negotiations with one of the world's poorest countries.

Notice, though, that it took that global protest, and the realization that it was potentially losing billions of turnover from bad publicity, before Nestlé conceded there was anything odd about what it was doing. Should companies have ethical standards that temper the capitalist mantra of the maximization of profits? Nestlé has a history of involvement in other issues that have given rise to international campaigns, such as formula milk for babies, cocoa and bottled water production, or child labour. Does this apparent indifference represent the other side of Swiss political neutrality which perhaps extends to ethical neutrality? The positive take-away that can be drawn from this history is that it is clear that such companies, wherever they operate, are today expected to behave by the highest ethical and environmental standards, not by what they can get away with locally.

Odium is frequently heaped on the institutions that have facilitated the process of globalization, particularly the World Bank, the International Monetary Fund, and the World Trade Organization (WTO), though sometimes this can involve not much more than an unsubstantiated rhetorical gesture. The objection to the World Bank is that it tends to make stringent conditions that conform to its own precepts of what is economically desirable, not those of the country itself. This is exacerbated by the fact that it works with governments rather than the people. Again and again, its grand schemes have been criticized because the local people affected are not sufficiently involved. The WTO, for its part, is often criticized for facilitating entry for Western or transnational companies into other markets on the best terms, while ensuring that the favour is not reciprocated the other way around, and doing nothing to alleviate the sinking price paid for commodities to the non-Western world.

Sharing resources in an unequal world

The world is rich and the world is poor. The world's population lives their lives somewhere along the long-drawn-out spectrum from poverty to riches. The nation-states of the world constitute a vast system of inequality, of unequal access to resources and commodities. The *Scientific American* has reported that a child born in the United States will create thirteen times as much ecological damage over the course of his or her lifetime as a child born in Brazil. Although globalization has, according to economists, lifted millions of people out of poverty, it is worth remembering that the definition of what, or how little, constitutes poverty has also been changed in the process.

You can analyse the class-income differences within countries, which globalization has increased very significantly, as we saw earlier with reference to the USA. One result has been unstable, populist politics and a veer to the political right. Or you can move up the scale to look at the differences between one country and another. The GNI (average annual income) figures make up a lengthy hierarchical table, a kind of class hierarchy of nations. Significantly, in the context of the present book, it is worth noting that we now have to go down to number seven in the list before we come to a Western country, Luxembourg (in the first edition of this book, it came at the top). At the head now is Qatar, where the annual income is $128,050 per person. At the bottom of this table is Burundi, with $730 per person.

These are the differences that have generated global action in different forms against the capitalist economic system in which we all live. However, with the ongoing destruction of the whole ecosystem of our planet increasingly evident to everyone as the climate, like politics, becomes more extreme and unstable, for many people the environment has overtaken inequality as their primary concern. Yet they are the two sides of the same coin.

Chapter 10
Ecology and indigeneity

In the forty or so years since it emerged as a field of study and activist philosophy, postcolonialism has itself pursued its own transformative trajectory. It's already been noted that the emphasis on its study of colonialism has shifted in emphasis from colonial history of exploitation in colonies such as India to settler colonies where the colonists themselves were the ones who achieved independence, as in the Americas. This has led to an increasing focus on the relation between settlers and the indigenous peoples of settler colonies, who lived on in what had formerly been their own territories under white colonial rule and even today often exist on very different terms from those of the mainstream societies of which they form a part.

The title of Frantz Fanon's *The Wretched of the Earth*, whether in English or its original French, *Les Damnés de la terre*, speaks tellingly of 'the earth': this awareness of human beings' relation to the earth on which they live, to the very material, earth, of which it is made, forms part of a fundamental orientation towards not just social justice but also an equitable relation to the environment which makes everyone's life possible. Here Fanon meets Gandhi. The concern for ecology, particularly in the context of environmental destruction by modern industrial capitalism and its products, together with its need to exploit natural resources to make noxious products such as plastic, has also led to a different awareness of the richness of the traditions of indigenous people who have often retained the knowledge and practices of lives that have little or no negative impact on the environment around them.

Who has the right to call themselves indigenous can be a highly political matter, as in Israel/Palestine. There is no agreed definition of the term, even in the landmark UN Declaration of the Rights of Indigenous Peoples of 2007, which marked a major political transformation when the declaration of indigenous rights was adopted by the UN General Assembly. In practice, the term indigenous in English (the French *indigène* by contrast has derogatory, colonial implications) is usually employed to describe relatively small groups of ethnically and culturally cohesive people who assert an ancestral relation to the land on which they have lived since earliest times. Typically, they may have few formal or legal rights to this land, because colonial law, that is European law, has only recently begun to recognize the validity of local precolonial customary law. Indigenous peoples, sometimes referred to as the 'fourth world', can be found on all continents—to cite just a few examples, the San (formerly called Bushmen) in South Africa, the Ma'dan (Marsh Arabs) some of whom still live in Iraq, the Adivasi or Naga peoples in South Asia, the Kavalan in Taiwan, the Ainu in Japan, the Sami in the Circumpolar North or Arctic, together with larger groups such as the Amazigh (formerly called Berbers) in North Africa, Aboriginal Australians, the Māori of New Zealand, as well as the seventy million or so indigenous peoples of the Americas who between them speak over 1,000 languages. In the Americas, many indigenous political groups identify their marginalized positions in opposition to contemporary forces of economic and industrial globalization, and survive as *campesinos*, small-scale farmers, or in some regions such as the Amazon as hunter-gatherers.

Indigenous politics tends to emphasize a fundamental relation to nature and the land, most publicly asserted when the first indigenous President of Bolivia, Evo Morales, instigated the *Ley de Derechos de la Madre Tierra* (The Law of the Rights of Mother Earth) in 2009. Although it has been less clear whether Morales himself continued to follow that path, indigenous politics often asserts the possibility of living a way of life that does not deplete resources or destroy the ecosystem. Indigenous knowledges are oriented in a fundamentally different way to traditional European ones: instead of seeking to triumph over nature, the basis of Western science and technology since the 18th century, human beings are rather understood as a part of the wider natural ecosphere in which they live, with the result that they establish a relation of care and respect for their environment which they seek to understand and draw on in non-destructive ways. The key concept and practice here is sustainability. In recent years, therefore, indigenous practices, far from being seen as 'primitive', non-modern, and in need of 'development', as used to be the case, have become exemplars for how to live and survive on this earth.

This is why indigeneity and ecology are so closely interlinked: it has often been indigenous peoples, such as the Ogoni peoples in Nigeria, who have campaigned most actively and effectively against the destructive intrusion of multinational corporations, in this case the oil companies, in their lands. As in the Amazon, it is the land and way of life of indigenous peoples that industrial resource extraction most often destroys.

It's in the broader context of deep ecology that some of what once seemed the more eccentric aspects of Gandhi's philosophy—his dislike of machinery, for example—have come to make more and more sense and continue to influence grass roots ecological politics in South Asia and elsewhere. Against the macho politics of huge development and infrastructure projects often pursued by male politicians since the days of Nasser in Egypt, such politics often form the basis of activism by women.

Take, for example, the Chipko movement in India, which was largely organized by women, and has been traced back directly by

Vandana Shiva to beginnings initiated by Mira Behn, one of the women closest to Gandhi. Shiva has argued that national colonization brought with it a colonization of living natural resources such as the forests, and then a mental colonization in its prescription of technological and market-oriented responses to farming and environmental issues. Resistance by peasants and tribals to the appropriation of forests began in the colonial period, when timber was exploited for military and industrial purposes without thought to the longer-term effects of deforestation and desertification or for the consequence of the destruction of closely interrelated local economies and ecologies.

In the late 1940s, Mira Behn moved to a farm in the foothills of the Himalayas. There she became increasingly concerned with the devastating annual flooding that occurred in the region, the causes of which, as she discovered, were both deforestation and the planting of new kinds of non-indigenous trees, particularly pines. Mira Behn established a new ashram, Gopal Ashram, in order to concentrate on the forest problem. She studied the local environment and, particularly, spent time acquiring knowledge about it from the local people who knew it intimately. Listening to their songs and folktales, Mira Behn noticed the many references to trees and plants that had more or less disappeared. She concluded that the ecological problems experienced in the area were the result of the disappearance of the forests of oak (*banj*). Whereas oak contributed positively to the ecological environment and the local economy, the pine, which had been more recently planted for purely commercial reasons, was an evergreen that contributed nothing to the local ecological economy, providing only cash crops of resin and wood pulp.

As the movement grew, a significant division developed which was essentially a gendered one. Initially the focus of many local organizations was on establishing cooperatives and asserting the rights of local people rather than big companies to exploit the wood of the forest as a commercial cash-crop. This, Shiva suggests, was essentially a masculist perspective. The women, who were responsible for cultivation of food crops and for fetching fuel and fodder, were not seduced by short-term advantages of monocultural cash crops. They rather emphasized the need for a sustainable local ecology in which vegetation, soil, and water formed a complex interrelated ecosystem. The divisions, therefore, were not only between the outsiders and the locals, but between the women and the men of the villages. The women challenged the principles of the whole system, charging that the men had been ideologically colonized by the short-term commercial values of the marketplace, trying to take control of nature just as patriarchy tries to control women. The women's perspective was not driven by the prospect of immediate gain through employing science to dominate nature but by the objective of a supportive, self-renewing forest system that preserved water and food resources. Their long-standing role of being the cultivators, of producing sustenance enabling their families to survive within this system, meant that the women possessed repositories of intimate knowledge both of husbandry and of the medicinal and nutritional value of a wide variety of plants.

It was therefore women who provided the foundation of the Chipko movement. It began in 1972–3 in the Chamoli district of north-west India, when local people successfully organized in order to protest against the sale by auction of 300 ash trees to a sports-goods manufacturer. By contrast, the local cooperative, which wanted to make agricultural implements, was forbidden by the government to cut even a small number of trees. The movement spread to other districts, such as Karnataka, and soon there was widespread resistance to the felling of forest trees that had been sold to commercial companies. Chipko means 'hugging': the name invoked a method first employed by the Bishnoi community in Rajasthan 300 years before. The Bishnoi, led by Amrita Devi, resisted the felling of their sacred *khejri* trees by embracing them (Figure 14), and gave up their lives in the struggle. In fact, there have been few modern instances where

14. Chipko tree-huggers, northern India, 1997.

villagers have literally hugged the trees to prevent the axe-men from cutting them down. The name of the movement, however, always works to suggest that in the last instance its activists may resort to hugging, as they have on occasion threatened. The idea of hugging trees also represents powerfully at a symbolic level the relationship of the people to the trees amongst which they live. In the face of increased landslides and flooding, activists in the Chipko movement pushed the campaign to a more radical level and began to agitate for a complete ban on the commercial exploitation of all of the forests in Uttar Pradesh, and subsequently campaigned against central government development projects initiated with little understanding of local needs and the local environment.

These campaigns were formed and carried out by local grassroots organizations; the Chipko movement was the product of collectives of activists. Together they achieved widespread and remarkable successes in preventing deforestation in their own areas throughout the Garhwal Himalayas. From then on, the Chipko movement moved deliberately towards the conservation of the forest as an ecosystem as well as a social system. Gradually, the focus on the preservation of forestation developed into a wider political philosophy of a sustainable ecology that formed a central part of local community values. This involves the pursuit of justice, of moral principles that are higher than those utilized by governments, of non-violent methods in relation to the environment as well as the community, of self-sufficiency and the empowerment of local knowledges: a resistance to centralization, corruption, exploitation, deprivation, hunger. An end to the split between private ethics of the family and the public ethos of the values of the marketplace.

The Chipko movement holds that forestation programmes run by central or state government bureaucrats based on the criteria of forest science destroy both the diversity of the forest ecoculture and the resource of commons and forest as a provider of food, fuel, building materials, medicines, for local people. A typical example of how this works would be the disregard of local species of trees and the widespread planting of a single non-indigenous species, such as Australian eucalyptus, which produces no humus and therefore fails to conserve water in the soil, destroying the earth's food system that supports plant, animal, and human life. Colonization of common land through privatization, and colonization through the introduction of exotic tree species, work in the same direction against the interests of local people, making their lives literally unsustainable by taking away their means of livelihood. Moreover, such schemes are usually administered through local bureaucratic organizations, which propel the local peasantry into the clutches of a corrupt alliance of the forces of power, privilege, and property.

Since the 1970s, the struggles of women, local villagers, and tribals in Chamoli, Karnataka, Jharkhand, and elsewhere have successfully arrested many of these practices and projects, as well as enabling the formulation of a whole environmental political philosophy. Vandana Shiva and other ecofeminists have pushed these fundamental principles further towards a critique of the practices of what they call 'maldevelopment', the industrial-development model which they characterize as a neo-colonial imposition. Such 'development' is typically organized at a state level, with international funding from the World Bank, and carried out according to the latest Western ideas of what crops (genetically modified) or trees should be grown, what (chemical) fertilizers used. Market-oriented ideas of how local land should be redistributed focus on the few who are able to take on substantial debt for land purchase, while the common land on which the poorest depend for food and fuel is privatized. The many attested failures of these projects, either directly or in terms of the production of unanticipated destructive side effects, has led even development economists to take seriously the local knowledges so long rejected as primitive and lacking the status of 'real', 'scientific' knowledge. This unauthorized knowledge empowers a politics of resistance: resisting the centralized control of the postcolonial state, resisting ideological colonization of the ethics and practices of the marketplace, and, most literally, resisting the colonization of local land by exotic, unsuitable plant species.

These kinds of political struggles by peasant movements have gone on in many places in India and elsewhere, and women have often been at the forefront of them. It is in India that they have been developed most fully from what has been described as a feminist sustainable development framework. Examples such as the Chipko movement cannot be generalized to the level of a universal model: the conditions of hill and forest dwellers in India are clearly specific to a particular society, and the women of these communities cannot be the basis for a unitary category of woman, third-world or otherwise. Nevertheless, given that it is rural women supporting families who are most directly affected by any degradation of their environment, the gendered force of these struggles remains prominent. Different threats can often be countered with similar methods of activism. For example, the Narmada Bachao Andolan's (NBA) extraordinarily brave and persistent populist campaign against the Sardar Sarovar Dam (Figure 15), part of the vast Narmada Valley Development Project, which was initiated by Nehru in 1961 and is still ongoing, clearly operates according to analogous principles. Here, a vast infrastructural project, costing billions of rupees, has displaced 200,000 Adivasi villagers and nomadic forest dwellers at enormous human and environmental cost. The disregard for the people affected is callous in the extreme. After a long campaign, the NBA succeeded in getting the World Bank, which was funding the project, to withdraw on the grounds of its adverse human and environmental impact. Since then other sources of funding have been found and, despite the NBA's legal challenges, the project has resumed its desultory, demented, destructive course. The struggle continues.

Other comparable examples would include the Greenbelt Movement in Kenya started by Wangari Maathai in 1977 after she

15. 'Damn You Dam Makers': local women protest against the construction of the Narmada Dam, Maheshwar, India, 1999.

had listened to local women expressing their concerns at the degradation of their environment. Their complaints involved issues all too common for peasant peoples across the world: whereas they had formerly been able to collect firewood locally, they now had to travel for miles to find it; their seeds no longer produced adequate crops with the result that their children suffered from malnutrition; their sources of clean water had dried up. Wangari Maathai began a campaign of planting seedlings to grow trees that would provide firewood, shade, humus for crops, and prevent soil erosion. By 2000, over fifteen million trees had been planted. At the same time, she led opposition to the destruction of the forest for construction development and the planting of non-sustaining export crops. The Greenbelt Movement has now spread to other African countries and around the world. At a different level of scale, the destruction of the Amazon rainforest has increased so dramatically in the 21st century that movements of resistance have moved from the local to global environmental organizations such as Friends of the Earth,

Greenpeace, and the World Wildlife Fund. Ecology has been transformed: while always local, the devastating effects of the industrialization that initiated the Anthropocene have reached globally catastrophic proportions, which means that climate action has moved beyond the register of the postcolonial as such. Globalization has at least enabled the linking of local movements into internationally powerful campaigns. Climate change now constitutes an international political crisis, which national politicians in liberal democracies with their time frames focused only on the next election are ill-equipped to deal with. Globalization from below that contests the forces of ecological destruction, such as the Climate Strike, offers a powerful political strategy to push for constructive changes in our relation to the environment which sustains us.

Chapter 11
Translation

Translating—between cultures

The strategy of this book has been to introduce postcolonialism through examples supported by readable theoretical expositions of the many issues with which postcolonial thought and practice are concerned. At this point, I want to introduce a concept that helps to bring together some of the diverse questions and situations that we have encountered and make sense of the layered oppositional politics of the postcolonial: translation. Translation, of course, is not something abstract. Even when it is theorized, it will always refer ultimately to a practice, like postcolonialism itself.

Nothing comes closer to the central activity and political dynamic of postcolonialism than the concept of translation. It may seem that the apparently neutral, technical activity of translating a text from one language into another operates in a realm very distinct from the highly charged political landscapes of the postcolonial world. Even at a practical level, however, the links can be significant. Literally, according to its Latin etymology, translation means to carry or to bear across (though it is worth noting that this was not the word the Romans themselves used for translation, which requires a separate discussion). Its literal meaning is thus identical with that of metaphor, which, according to its Greek etymology, means to carry or to bear across. A colony begins as a translation, a copy of the original located elsewhere on the map. New England. New Spain. New Amsterdam. New York. Colonial clone. A far-away reproduction that will, inevitably, always turn out to be different.

Translation is also a kind of metaphorical displacement of a text from one language to another. If metaphor involves a version of translation, it is because, as the Ancient Greek philosopher Aristotle pointed out, a metaphor is using a literal meaning in a figurative sense, so that it is no longer empirically true: 'Darling. You're an angel!' To create a metaphor is to engineer a creative lie, by saying what an object is by saying what it is not. Even 'truth', the 19th-century German philosopher Nietzsche suggested radically, is just a metaphor that we have forgotten is a metaphor. We could say that postcolonial analysis is centrally concerned with these kinds of linguistic, cultural, and geographical transfer, transformations of positive and negative kinds: changing things into things which they are not. Or showing that they were never that way in the first place. Or that a neutral-sounding word is really a sleeping metaphor that means something else.

In the case of translation, this alteration is also literally true: to translate a text from one language to another is to transform its material identity. With colonialism, the transformation of an indigenous culture into the subordinated culture of a colonial regime or sovereign settler colony, or the superimposition of the colonial apparatus into which all aspects of the original culture have to be reconstructed, operate as processes of translational dematerialization and reconstruction. At the same time, though, certain aspects of the indigenous culture may remain untranslatable and endure. A translation always leaves a certain residue behind.

As a practice, translation begins as a matter of intercultural communication, but it also always involves questions of power relations and forms of domination. It cannot therefore avoid political issues, or questions about its own links to current institutions of power. No act of translation takes place in an entirely neutral space of absolute equality. Someone is translating something or someone. Someone or something is being translated, transformed from a subject to an object, like the Arab woman in the photograph in Chapter 7, Figure 9. The Spaniard who goes to North America finds herself translated from a first-world individual to a third-world Latina. The Ghanaian princess goes to the United States and finds that she has become a second-class citizen, treated as if she were just another African-American. The colonized person is also in the condition of being a translated man or woman, from citizen to subject.

Languages also exist in a hierarchy, like classes and nations: as does translation itself, traditionally thought of in terms of an original and an inferior copy. Under colonialism, the colonial copy can become more powerful than its original, as with the United States and the United Kingdom. In all cases, the indigenous original gets devalued as the copy of another metropolitan country is imposed upon it. It will even be claimed that the copy corrects deficiencies in the native version. The colonial language becomes culturally more powerful, devaluing the native language as it is brought into its domain, domesticated and accommodated. One of the initial acts of colonization was often to translate significant indigenous written and oral texts into the colonizer's language. In this way, translation transformed oral cultures into the webs and snares of writing, into what the Uruguayan critic Angel Rama calls 'the lettered city', a proliferation of writing which, unlike the social construction of oral cultures, would be accessible only to a privileged few. Translation becomes part of the process of domination, of achieving control, a violence carried out on the language, culture, and people being translated. The close links between colonization and translation begin not with acts of exchange, but with violence and appropriation, of 'deterritorialization'. As the Irish dramatist Brian Friel has shown in his play *Translations* (1981), the act of naming and renaming geographical features in a landscape also constituted an act of power and appropriation, often desacralizing, as in Ireland or in Australia, where mapping became the necessary adjunct of the incorporative processes of imperialism.

However, it would be a mistake to assume that even colonial translation was always a one-way process. Travellers and conquerors were frequently dependent on the services of translators, and relied on them for understanding almost everything about the native peoples whom they encountered. The literal meaning of a large number of places still on today's maps is something like 'I don't know what the name of this place is'. False translation has, for the most part, been considered under the framework of Orientalism, where it involves a representation of another culture without reference to the original, as, for example, in stereotyping, where the writer or artist even sometimes goes to the length of creating the image of what the colonizer expected to find—such as the fantasy of the colonial harem. False translation can also suggest the possibility of diplomacy and duplicity, what might be termed 'duplomacy', what the postcolonial theorist Homi K. Bhabha calls the 'sly civility' of different kinds of accommodation and evasion, often carried out as subtle everyday forms of resistance. This develops into a culture of lying, of the 'lying native', who translates him- or herself into the dominant culture by means of a mimicry that undoes the original, by being like it but not quite.

If translation involves the power structure of acts of appropriation, it can also invoke power through acts of resistance. In a sense, this comes closer to traditional ideas about translation. Here, the aphorism *'traduttore, traditore'*—translator, traitor—moves out of the realm of betrayal and reverses itself. Where the indigenous culture is being opened up for appropriation by the conquering culture, any accommodating translation involves an act of treachery; here the necessary, traditionally lamented failure of translation becomes a positive force of resistance, resisting the intruder.

There are other kinds of intruder: those who choose to migrate from the periphery to the centre. Translation becomes central to the migrant's experience in the metropolitan or postcolonial city, as she or he takes on the more active role of cultural translator. Having translated themselves, migrants then encounter other translated men and women, other restless marginals, and translate their experiences to each other to form new languages of desire and aspiration: circuits of activism, routes of affirmation.

The Caribbean has always been a space of translation as a two-way process, through its different languages and cultures. It even has its own term for it: creolization. As the word 'creole' implies, here translation involves displacement, the carrying over and transformation of the dominant culture into new identities that take on material elements from the culture of their new location. Both sides of the exchange get creolized, transformed, as a result, which may make their meanings less transparent. As the Martiniquan writer Édouard Glissant has elaborated, translation may also involve 'opacity', an untranslatability which resists the power of domination. Caribbean creolization can thus also involve a space of re-empowerment. How can such forms of empowering translation be activated?

Empowering Fanon

When you finally drive out from Algiers, from its long arcades, its dazzling sunlit sea and secret fragrances, you come in a little while to Boufarik. High in the air before you, on the wall of the factory of the Compagnie Française des Produits Orangina, shakes the blue and yellow logo of Orangina, the fizzy drink founded by a French settler in 1936, and now beloved of all those who find themselves anywhere enclosed in the searing, sealed volume of the summer heat of the Maghreb or the Mediterranean.

Ah! Orangina™!

Refreshed, you leave the lush orange groves and continue on to Blida, *la ville des roses,* another city of flowers, and of football, dominated by the bright turquoise dome of the mosque with its four tiled minarets, with the strange inhospitable Atlas Mountains towering dark cedar blue beyond.

A couple of miles beyond the city as you turn back from the steep gorges that rise above the vast Mitidja plain, the invisible dry scents of Aleppo pines finally give way to the moist, sweet smells of vineyards and orchards. You turn a corner in the road and see, in the distance, its high stone walls surrounded by huge wheat fields, the huge psychiatric hospital of Blida-Joinville. Its hundred or so buildings are laid out amongst landscaped walks, gardens, and rows of trees offering shade in the summer heat.

Inside a large, solid, stuccoed house, a young woman and her son play in the quiet of the afternoon. It is November 1953. A few hundred yards away, the new *chef de service* of psychiatry at the hospital stands with the single nurse in charge at the doorway of a ward in which he sees sixty-nine inmates, *indigènes*, natives, all chained to their beds in straitjackets. The forceful new *chef de service* stares angrily at the scene of quiet torture. In a re-enactment of Philippe Pinel's legendary act of unlocking the chains of the inmates at Paris's Salpêtrière Hospital at the time of the French Revolution, he orders the nurse to release them all. The nurse stares at him, uncomprehending. In a fury, the new chief shouts his order out more insistently. One by one, the straitjackets start to be undone, unpeeled like an orange.

The patients lie there without moving as Frantz Fanon (Figure 16) explains to them that there will be no more straitjackets, no more chains, no more segregation in the wards between settlers and natives, that henceforth the patients will live and work together as groups.

16. Frantz Fanon.

Perhaps nothing in Fanon's life so decisively represented his politics of translation as his dramatic entrance to the hospital at Blida-Joinville, transforming the patients from passive, victimized objects into subjects who began to recognize that they were in charge of their own destiny. From disempowerment to empowerment, from the degradations of the experiences recounted in *Black Skin, White Masks* to the revolutionary *Wretched of the Earth*.

Fanon's two best-known books are themselves about translation, or, more accurately, retranslation. In *Black Skin, White Masks*, he argues that the black man and woman have already been translated not only as colonial subjects in the regime of French imperialism, but also internally, psychologically: their desires have been changed into another form, carried across into a wish for whiteness through a kind of metempsychosis. Their very desires have been transposed, though they have never, of course, actually become white. They have black skins, with a white mask. But the problem is that the mask is not just a mask: it has been profoundly internalized into the furthest depths of the psyche.

Fanon's project is to understand this so as to find a way to translate himself back again. This begins with a refusal of translation, of black into the values of white. Like Freud's psychoanalysis, it involves a detranslation, as a result of the failure of translation. In the same way, in *Wretched of the Earth*, Fanon writes of how the indigenous person has been created as, translated by colonialism into, 'a native', and inscribed with the schizoculture of colonialism as its devalued other. He states,

> If psychiatry is the medical technique that aims to enable man no longer to be a stranger to his environment . . . I owe it to myself to affirm that the Arab, permanently an alien in his own country, lives in a state of absolute depersonalization. . . . The events in Algeria are the logical consequence of an abortive attempt to decerebralize a people.

Decerebralization: they have been dehumanized, made to see themselves as other, alienated from their own culture, language, land. In *Wretched of the Earth*, the task Fanon sets himself is the gaining of self-respect through revolutionary anti-colonial

147

violence, where violence for the colonized native is a form of disintoxication, self-translation, the act, the grasping of agency. As a doctor, Fanon was equally emphatic about the possibilities of auto-translation through a dynamic, dialogic model of education, a pedagogy of the oppressed, so that the translated became translators, activist writers. The subjects, not objects, of history. With Fanon, translation becomes a synonym for performative, activist writing, which seeks to produce direct bodily somatic effects on the reader—of which his own writing is one of the greatest examples.

Performers, players, human beings freed from their straitjackets, mental or physical. A short time after Fanon's arrival at Blida-Joinville, one afternoon the hospital's director phones the police in panic, shouting down the phone that there has been a break-out of at least ten inmates from the hospital, and that the new *chef de service* is missing as well. A couple of hours later, the director is somewhat abashed when the hospital bus returns with Fanon, exuberant, accompanied by his victorious hospital football team.

Three years later, Fanon would resign his position, on the grounds that it was impossible to cure with psychiatry the psychic wounds that were the direct result of the continued oppression of the French colonial system. The problem with his patients was not a childhood traumatic experience buried in their unconscious as Freud had assumed—it was the direct product of the social experience of a racist, authoritarian colonial society violently repressing an Algerian anti-colonial uprising. Fanon was ordered to leave Algeria within two days by the French authorities.

Fanon spent the rest of his short life with the Front de libération nationale (FLN), working tirelessly towards the ends of the political and social liberation of Algeria. As an engaged intellectual, Fanon demonstrated how important political interventions could be achieved by developing the connections between his intellectual work, his medical practice, and his collective political activism. Postcolonialism remains irrevocably haunted and inspired by his analytical work and his impassioned example, as translator, empowerer, liberator.

References

Sources of specific references in the text are given below. Other sources and suggestions for further reading will be found in the next section.

Introduction: montage

Edward W. Said (1978), *Orientalism: Western Representations of the Orient* (Harmondsworth: Penguin, 1985)

Samuel P. Huntingdon, *The Clash of Civilizations and the Remaking of the World Order* (New York: Simon and Schuster, 1996)

Global South economies: https://www.focus-economics.com/blog/the-largest-economies-in-the-world

Wealth gap in USA: https://www.forbes.com/sites/noahkirsch/2017/11/09/the-3-richest-americans-hold-more-wealth-than-bottom-50-of-country-study-finds/#6bcc52e83cf8

Ngũgĩ wa Thiong'o, *Decolonizing the Mind: The Politics of Language in African Literature* (London: James Currey, 1986)

Montage, fragments: Walter Benjamin, 'Theses on the Philosophy of History', in *Illuminations*, trans. H. Zohn (London: Fontana, 1973)

Chapter 1: Subaltern knowledges

You find yourself a refugee

Oral communications

Tara Zahra, *The Great Departure* (New York: Norton: 2016)

Hannah Arendt, 'We Refugees', in *The Jewish Writings* ed. Jerome Kohn and Ron H. Feldman (New York: Schocken Books, 2007)

Lyndsey Stonebridge, *Placeless People* (Oxford: Oxford University Press, 2018)

Different kinds of knowledge

Bare life: Giorgio Agamben, *Homo Sacer: Sovereign Power and Bare Life*, trans. Daniel Heller-Roazen (Stanford: Stanford University Press, 1998)

James Joyce, *Ulysses: The 1922 Text* (New York: Oxford University Press, 2007)

'Learning under Shelling', http://www.poica.org/

Bloke Modisane, *Blame Me on History* (London: Penguin, 1990)

Knowledge, politics, and power

Hannah Arendt, *On Violence* (New York: Harcourt, 1970)

Amilcar Cabral, *Return to the Source. Selected Speeches by Amilcar Cabral* (New York: Monthly Review Press, 1973)

Michel Foucault, *'Society Must Be Defended': Lectures at the Collège de France, 1975–1976*, trans. David Macey (New York: Picador, 1993)

The subaltern and the subaltern woman

Ranajit Guha, 'Preface', *Subaltern Studies I: Writings on South Asian History and Society* (Delhi: Oxford University Press, 1982), pp. vii–viii

Gayatri Chakravorty Spivak, 'Can the Subaltern Speak?', in *Marxism and the Interpretation of Culture*, eds Carys Nelson and Lawrence Grossberg (Basingstoke: Macmillan 1988), pp. 271–313

Assia Djebar, *Fantasia: An Algerian Cavalcade*, trans. Dorothy S. Blair (Portsmouth, NH: Heinemann, 1993)

Tony Morrison, *Beloved* (New York: Vintage, 1987)

Languages

Tsitsi Dangarembega, *Nervous Conditions* (London: The Women's Press, 1988)

Gloria Anzaldúa, *The Gloria Anzaldúa Reader*, ed. AnaLouise Keating (Durham: Duke University Press, 2009)

Abdelkabir Khatibi, *Plural Maghreb: Writings on Postcolonialism*, trans. P. Burcu Yalim (London: Bloomsbury Academic, 2019)

Literatures

Albert Memmi (1957), *The Colonizer and the Colonized*, trans. Howard Greenfeld (Boston: Beacon Press, 1965)

Bill Ashcroft, Gareth Griffiths, and Helen Tiffin, *The Empire Writes Back* (London: Routledge, 1989)

Abdelfattah Kilito, *Thou Shalt Not Speak My Language*, trans. Wail S. Hassan (Syracuse: Syracuse University Press, 2008)

Chapter 2: Colonialisms, decolonization, decoloniality

Indigenous deaths in South America: David P. Forsythe, *Encyclopedia of Human Rights*, Volume 4 (Oxford: Oxford University Press, 2009), p. 297

Mauricio Tenorio-Trillo, *Latin America: The Allure and Power of an Idea* (Chicago: Chicago University Press, 2017)

Decoloniality

Walter Mignolo, *Local Histories/Global Designs: Coloniality, Subaltern Knowledges, and Border Thinking* (Princeton: Princeton University Press, 2012)

Walter Mignolo and Catherine Walsh, *On Decoloniality: Concepts, Analytics, Praxis* (Durham: Duke University Press, 2018)

'The great divergence': Robert C. Allen, *Global Economic History: A Very Short Introduction* (Oxford: Oxford University Press, 2011)

Michel Foucault (1961), *History of Madness*, ed. Jean Khalfa (New York: Routledge, 2006)

Max Horkheimer and Theodor W. Adorno, *Dialectic of Enlightenment*, trans. John Cumming (New York: Continuum, 1982)

Chapter 3: Slavery, race, caste

Race and racism

Cedric Robinson, *Black Marxism: The Making of the Black Radical Tradition* (London: Zed Press, 1983)

Paul Gilroy, *The Black Atlantic: Modernity and Double Consciousness* (London: Verso, 1993)

Lisa Lowe, *The Intimacies of Four Continents* (Durham: Duke University Press, 2015)

Frantz Fanon, *Black Skin, White Masks*, trans. Richard Philcox (New York: Grove Press, 2008)

Ralph Ellison, *Invisible Man* (New York: Random House, 1952)

W. E. B. Du Bois, *Writings* (New York: Library of America, 1986)

Caste

www.dalits.org

Aniket Jaaware, *Practicing Caste: On Touching and Not Touching* (New York: Fordham University Press, 2018)

B. R. Ambedkar (1936) 'Annihilation of Caste', http://www.ambedkar.org/ambcd/02.Annihilation%20of%20Caste.htm

Caste and British colonialism: Mulk Raj Anand (1935), *Untouchable* (Harmondsworth: Penguin Books, 1940)

Chapter 4: History and power, from below and above

Bombing Iraq—since 1920

Oral communications

Chapter 5: Nomads, nation-states, borders

Nomads

Terra nullius: Locke in fact never uses the term, but the general reference is to the second of his *Two Treatises of Government*, ed. Peter Laslett (Cambridge: Cambridge University Press, 1988)

Nomadism: Gilles Deleuze and Félix Guattari, *A Thousand Plateaus: Capitalism and Schizophrenia*, Vol. II, trans. Brian Massumi (London: Athlone, 1988)

Movimento sem terra (MST) website: http://www.mstbrazil.org/

Nation-states

Robert J. C. Young, *Empire, Colony, Postcolony* (Oxford: Wiley-Blackwell, 2015), pp. 66–84

Unsettled states: nations and their borders

Martin Lloyd, *The Passport: The History of Man's Most Travelled Document* (Thrupp: Sutton Publishing, 2003)

Leela Gandhi, *Affective Communities: Anticolonial Thought, Fin-de-Siècle Radicalism, and the Politics of Friendship* (Durham: Duke University Press, 2006)

Benedict Anderson, *Imaginary Communities: Reflections on the Origin and Spread of Nationalism* (London: Verso, 1983)

Benedict Anderson, *The Spectre of Comparisons: Nationalism, Southeast Asia, and the World* (London: Verso, 1998)

Rabindranath Tagore (1916), *Home and the World*, trans.
Surendranath Tagore (London: Penguin, 1985)

Virginia Woolf, *Three Guineas* (New York: Harcourt, 1938)

The wall

Roy Moxham, *The Great Hedge of India* (London: Constable, 2001)

Film: *Touch of Evil*, dir. Orson Welles (1958)

Chapter 6: Hybridity

Frantz Fanon, *Black Skin, White Masks*, trans. Richard Philcox
(New York: Grove Press, 2008)

Homi K. Bhabha, *The Location of Culture* (London:
Routledge, 1994)

Salman Rushdie, *Imaginary Homelands: Essays and Criticism
1981–1991* (London: Granta, 1991)

Édouard Glissant, *The Poetics of Relation*, trans. Betsy Wing (Ann
Arbor, MI: University of Michigan Press, 1997)

Fernando Ortiz, *Cuban Counterpoint: Tobacco and Sugar*, trans.
Harriet de Onís (Durham: Duke University Press, 1995)

Raï and Islamic social space

Philip V. Bohlman, *World Music: A Very Short Introduction* (Oxford:
Oxford University Press, 2002)

Homi K. Bhabha, 'The Third Space: Interview with Homi K. Bhabha',
in Jonathan Rutherford, ed., *Identity: Community, Culture,
Difference* (London: Lawrence & Wishart, 1990)

Cheb Khaled: Marc Schade-Poulsen, *Men and Popular Music in
Algeria* (Austin: University of Texas Press, 1999)

Chapter 7: The ambivalence of the veil

Edward W. Said (1978), *Orientalism: Western Representations of the
Orient* (Harmondsworth: Penguin, 1985)

Film: *Battle of Algiers*, dir. Gillo Pontecorvo (1965)

Frantz Fanon, 'Algeria Unveiled', in *A Dying Colonialism*, trans.
Haakon Chevalier (New York: Grove Press, 1965)

Fadwa El Guindi, *Veil: Modesty, Privacy and Resistance* (Oxford:
Berg, 1999)

Chapter 8: Gender, queering, and feminism in a postcolonial context

Gayatri Chakravorty Spivak, 'Can the Subaltern Speak?', in *Marxism and the Interpretation of Culture*, eds Carys Nelson and Lawrence Grossberg (Basingstoke: Macmillan, 1988), pp. 271–313

Arundhati Roy, *The Algebra of Infinite Justice* (London: Flamingo, 2002)

M. K. Gandhi, *Hind Swaraj, and Other Writings*, ed. Anthony J. Parel (Cambridge: Cambridge University Press, 1997)

Women's movements after independence

Amina al-Sa'id, 'The Role of Women Does Not End with Peace', *Hawa' al gadida* 24 December 1956

What makes postcolonial feminism 'postcolonial'?

Simone de Beauvoir and Gisèle Halimi, *Djamila Boupacha*, trans. Peter Green (London: André Deutsch, Weidenfeld, and Nicolson, 1962)

Phoolan Devi, *I, Phoolan Devi: The Autobiography of India's Bandit Queen* (London: Little, Brown & Co, 1996)

Film: *Bandit Queen*, dir. Shekhar Kapur (1995)

Chapter 9: Globalization from a postcolonial perspective

Che reads *The Wretched of the Earth*

John Lee Anderson, *Che Guevara: A Revolutionary Life* (New York: Grove Press, 2010)

Josie Fanon interview: *Che Guevara Speaks*, ed. Steve Clark (Pathfinder Press, 2000), pp. 129–33

Che Guevara, 'Socialism and Man in Cuba' (1965), in Ernesto Che Guevara, *Che Guevara Reader: Writings on Guerrilla Strategy, Politics and Revolution*, ed. David Deutschmann (Melbourne: Ocean Press, 1997), pp. 212–30

François Maspero, 'Hommages à Frantz Fanon', *Présence Africaine* 40, 1962

Francis Jeanson, 'Preface', *Peau noir, masques blancs* (Paris: Seuil, 1952)

Frantz Fanon, *Toward the African Revolution*, trans. Haakon Chevalier (New York: Monthly Review Press, 1967)

Aimé Césaire, 'Hommages à Frantz Fanon', *Présence Africaine* 40, 1962

Globalization

Marshall McLuhan and Quentin Fiore, *War and Peace in the Global Village* (New York: Bantam Books, 1968)

World Bank reports and data: http://www.worldbank.org/

'Nestlé Claims £3.7m from Famine-Hit Ethiopia', *Guardian*, 19 December 2002

Why Nestlé is one of the most hated companies in the world: https://www.zmescience.com/science/nestle-company-pollution-children/#Baby_Formula_and_Boycott

The Financial Times, 21 December 2003

Sharing resources in an unequal world

Ecological damage: 'Use It and Lose It: The Outsize Effect of U.S. Consumption on the Environment', https://www.scientificamerican.com/article/american-consumption-habits/

World GNI by country: Ferdinand, Bada, 'Countries by GNI per Capita', WorldAtlas, 3 April 2019, worldatlas.com/articles/countries-by-gni-per-capita.html

Chapter 10: Ecology and indigeneity

Frantz Fanon, *The Wretched of the Earth*, trans. Richard Philcox (New York: Grove Press, 2004)

UN Declaration of the Rights of Indigenous Peoples: https://www.un.org/development/desa/indigenouspeoples/declaration-on-the-rights-of-indigenous-peoples.html

The Law of the Rights of Mother Earth: http://www.worldfuturefund.org/Projects/Indicators/motherearthbolivia.html

Feminism and ecology

Vandana Shiva, *Staying Alive: Women, Ecology and Survival in India* (New Delhi: Kali for Women, 1988)

Chapter 11: Translation

Translating—between cultures

Friedrich Nietzsche, *Philosophy and Truth*: *Selections from Nietzsche's Notebooks of the Early 1870's*, trans. Daniel Breazeale (Atlantic Highlands, NJ: Humanities Press, 1979)

Angel Rama, *The Lettered City*, trans. John Charles Chasteen (Durham: Duke University Press, 1996)

Frantz Fanon, *The Wretched of the Earth*, trans. Richard Philcox (New York: Grove Press, 2004)

Brian Friel, *Translations* (London: Faber, 1981)

Malek Alloula, *The Colonial Harem* (Manchester: Manchester University Press, 1987)

Homi K. Bhabha, '*Sly Civility*': *The Location of Culture* (London: Routledge, 1994)

Édouard Glissant, *Poetics of Relation*, trans. Betsy Wing (Ann Arbor, MI: University of Michigan Press, 1997)

Empowering Fanon

Frantz Fanon, *Toward the African Revolution*, trans. Haakon Chevalier (New York: Monthly Review Press, 1967)

Further reading

Introduction: montage

Postcolonialism's relation to the anti-colonial movements:
Robert J. C. Young, *Postcolonialism: An Historical Introduction*,
2nd ed. (Oxford: Blackwell, 2016)
Two Indian introductions to postcolonial theory: Leela Gandhi,
Postcolonial Theory: A Critical Introduction (Edinburgh:
Edinburgh University Press, 1998); Ania Loomba, *Colonialism/
Postcolonialism* (Abingdon: Routledge, 2015)
Edward W. Said, *Culture and Imperialism* (London: Chatto &
Windus, 1993)

Chapter 1: Subaltern knowledges

You find yourself a refugee

Michel Agier, *Managing the Undesirables: Refugee Camps and
Humanitarian Government* (Cambridge: Polity Press, 2011)
Jeremy Harding, *Border Vigils: Keeping Migrants out of the Rich
World* (London: Verso, 2012)
Elisabeth Leake, *The Defiant Border: The Afghan-Pakistan
Borderlands in the Era of Decolonization, 1936–1965* (Cambridge:
Cambridge University Press, 2016)
Peter Tinti and Tuesday Reitano, *Migrant, Refugee, Smuggler, Saviour*
(London: Hurst, 2016)

Different kinds of knowledge

Dipesh Chakrabarty, *Provincializing Europe: Postcolonial Thought and Historical Difference* (Princeton, NJ: Princeton University Press, 2000)

Vinay Lal, *Empire of Knowledge: Culture and Plurality in the Global Economy* (London: Pluto Press, 2002)

Achille Mbembe, *On the Postcolony* (Berkeley, CA: University of California Press, 2001)

Linda Tuhiwei Smith, *Decolonizing Methodologies: Research and Indigenous Peoples* (London: Zed Books, 1999)

Knowledge, politics, and power

Michel Foucault, *Power/Knowledge: Selected Interviews and Other Writings, 1972–1977*, trans. Colin Gordon (New York: Vintage, 1980)

Gillian Rose, *Feminism and Geography: The Limits of Geographical Knowledge* (Cambridge: Polity Press, 1993)

Edward W. Said, *Covering Islam: How the Media and the Experts Determine How We See the Rest of the World* (New York: Vintage Books, 1997)

Immanuel Wallerstein, *The Modern World System*, 3 vols (New York: Academic Press, 1974–89)

The subaltern and the subaltern woman

Trinh T. Minh-ha, *Woman, Native, Other: Writing Postcoloniality and Feminism* (Bloomington, IN: Indiana University Press, 1989)

José David Saldívar, *Trans-Americanity: Subaltern Modernities, Global Coloniality, and the Cultures of Greater Mexico* (Durham, NC: Duke University Press, 2012)

Languages

Monica Heller and Bonnie McElhinny, *Language, Capitalism, Colonialism: Toward a Critical History* (Toronto: University of Toronto Press, 2017)

Robert J. C. Young, 'That which is Casually Called a Language', *PMLA* 131.5 (2016), pp. 1207–21.

Literatures

Emily Apter, *Against World Literature: On the Politics of Untranslatability* (London: Verso, 2013)

Elleke Boehmer, *Colonial and Postcolonial Literatures*, 2nd ed. (Oxford: Oxford University Press, 2005)

Neil Lazarus, *The Postcolonial Unconscious* (Cambridge: Cambridge University Press, 2011)

Chapter 2: Colonialisms, decolonization, decoloniality

Jerry Brotton, *A History of the World in Twelve Maps* (New York: Penguin Books, 2014)

Aimé Césaire, *Discourse on Colonialism*, trans Joan Pinkham (New York: Monthly Review Press, 2001)

Peter Frankopan, *The Silk Roads: A New History of the World* (New York Vintage 2015)

Anne McClintock, *Imperial Leather: Race, Gender and Sexuality in the Colonial Contest* (New York: Routledge, 1995)

Ashis Nandy, *Intimate Enemy: Loss and Recovery of Self under Colonialism* (Delhi: Oxford University Press, 1983)

Lorenzo Veracini, *Settler Colonialism: A Theoretical Overview* (Basingstoke: Palgrave Macmillan, 2010)

Robert J. C. Young, 'Postcolonial Remains', *New Literary History* 43.1 (2012), pp. 19–42.

Decoloniality

Fernando Coronil, *The Fernando Coronil Reader: The Struggle for Life Is the Matter*, eds Julie Skurski et al. (Durham, NC: Duke University Press, 2018)

Boaventura de Sousa Santos, *Epistemologies of the South: Justice against Epistemicide* (New York: Routledge, 2014)

Nelson Maldonado-Torres, *Against War: Views from the Underside of Modernity* (Durham, NC: Duke University Press, 2008)

Walter Mignolo, *The Darker Side of Western Modernity* (Durham, NC: Duke University Press, 2011)

Anibal Quijano, 'Coloniality and Modernity/Rationality', *Cultural Studies* 21.2–3 (2007), pp. 168–78.

For the internationalist tradition, see: Anne Garland Mahler, *From the Tricontinental to the Global South: Race, Radicalism, and Transnational Solidarity* (Durham, NC: Duke University Press, 2018)

Chapter 3: Slavery, race, caste

Race and racism

George M. Fredrickson, *Racism: A Short History* (Princeton, NJ: Princeton University Press, 2015)

Achille Mbembe, 'Necropolitics', *Public Culture*, 15.1 (2003), pp. 11–40

Laura Ann Stoler, *Race and the Education of Desire: Foucault's History of Sexuality and the Colonial Order of Things* (Durham, NC: Duke University Press, 1995)

Robert J. C. Young, *Colonial Desire: Hybridity in Culture, Theory and Race* (London: Routledge, 1995)

Caste

Robert Deliège, *The Untouchables of India* (Oxford: Berg, 1999)

Anupama Rao, *The Caste Question* (Berkeley, CA: University of California Press, 2009)

Suraj Yengde, *Caste Matters* (Delhi: Penguin, 2019)

Chapter 4: History and power, from below and above

Bombing Iraq—since 1920

James Barr, *A Line in the Sand: Britain, France, and the Struggle that Shaped the Middle East* (New York: Simon and Schuster, 2012)

Charles Tripp, *A History of Iraq*, 3rd ed. (Cambridge: Cambridge University Press, 2007)

Chapter 5: Nomads, nation-states, borders

Andro Linklater, *Owning the Earth: The Transforming History of Land Ownership* (London: Bloomsbury, 2014)

Doreen Massey, *For Space* (London: Sage Publications, 2005)

Simón Ventura Trujillo, *Land Uprising: Native Story Power and the Insurgent Horizons of Latinx Indigeneity* (Tucson: University of Arizona Press, 2020)

Nation-states

Homi K. Bhabha, ed., *Nation and Narration* (London: Routledge, 1990)

Eric Hobsbawm, *Nations and Nationalism since 1870: Programme, Myth, Reality* (Cambridge: Cambridge University Press, 1990)

Kumari Jayawardena, *Feminism and Nationalism in the Third World* (London: Zed Books, 1986)

James C. Scott, *Seeing Like a State: How Certain Schemes to Improve the Human Condition Have Failed* (New Haven: Yale University Press, 1998)

Edward Weisband and Courtney I. P. Thomas, *Political Culture and the Making of Modern Nation-States* (New York: Routledge, 2015)

Unsettled states: nations and their borders

Joe Cleary, *Literature, Partition and the Nation-state: Culture and Conflict in Ireland, Israel and Palestine* (Cambridge: Cambridge University Press, 2002)

Amitav Ghosh, *The Shadow Lines* (London: Bloomsbury, 1988)

Ian Lustick, *Unsettled States, Disputed Lands: Britain and Ireland, France and Algeria, Israel and the West Bank-Gaza* (Ithaca, NY: Cornell University Press, 1993)

Mahmood Mamdani, *Citizen and Subject: Contemporary Africa and the Legacy of Late Colonialism* (London: James Currey, 1996)

The wall

Néstor Garcia Canclini, *Hybrid Cultures: Strategies for Entering and Leaving Modernity*, trans. Christopher L. Chiappari and Silvia L. López (Minneapolis: University of Minnesota Press, 1995)

Cetta Mainwaring, *At Europe's Edge: Migration and Crisis in the Mediterranean* (Oxford: Oxford University Press, 2019)

Todd Miller, *Storming the Wall: Climate Change, Migration, and Homeland Security* (San Francisco: City Lights, 2017)

Joseph Nevins, *Operation Gatekeeper and Beyond*, 2nd ed. (New York: Routledge, 2010)

Chapter 6: Hybridity

Raï and Islamic social space

Hisham Aidi, *Rebel Music—Race, Empire, and the New Muslim Youth Culture* (New York: Pantheon, 2014)

Jon Lusk and S. Broughton (eds.), *The Rough Guide to World Music*, Vol. 1 (London: Penguin, 2006)

Luis Martinez, *The Algerian Civil War 1990–1998* (London: Hurst, 2000)

Chapter 7: The ambivalence of the veil

David C. Gordon, *Women of Algeria: An Essay on Change* (Cambridge, MA: Harvard University Press, 1968)

Sarah Graham-Brown, *Images of Women: The Portrayal of Women in Photography of the Middle East, 1860–1950* (London: Quartet, 1988)

Neil MacMaster, *Burning the Veil: The Algerian War and the 'Emancipation' of Muslim Women, 1954–62* (Manchester: Manchester University Press, 2010)

Subcomandante Marcos, *Shadows of Tender Fury: The Letters and Communiqués of Subcomandante Marcos and the Zapatista Army of National Liberation* (New York: Monthly Review Press, 1995)

Chapter 8: Gender, queering, and feminism in a postcolonial context

Arnaldo Cruz-Malavé and Martin F. Manalansan, eds, *Queer Globalizations: Citizenship and the Afterlife of Colonialism* (New York: New York University Press, 2002)

John C. Hawley, ed., *Postcolonial, Queer: Theoretical Intersections* (Albany: State University of New York Press, 2001)

Ania Loomba, *Revolutionary Desires: Women, Communism, and Feminism in India* (New York: Routledge 2018)

Joseph A. Massad, *Desiring Arabs* (Chicago: University of Chicago Press, 2007)

Chandra Talpade Mohanty, Ann Russo, and Lourdes Torres, eds, *Third World Women and the Politics of Feminism* (Bloomington, IN: Indiana University Press, 1991)

Pedro Paulo Gomes Pereira, *Queer in the Tropics: Gender and Sexuality in the Global South* (Cham: Springer, 2019)

Women's movements after independence

Hind Wassef and Nadia Wassef, eds, *Daughters of the Nile: Photographs of Egyptian Women's Movements, 1900–1960* (Cairo: The American University in Cairo Press, 2001)

What makes postcolonial feminism 'postcolonial'?

Leila Ahmed, *Women and Gender in Islam: Historical Roots of a Modern Debate* (New Haven: Yale University Press, 1992)

Gisèle Halimi, *Avocate irrespectueuse* (Paris: Plon, 2002)

Saba Mahmoud, *Politics of Piety: The Islamic Revival and the Feminist Subject* (Princeton, NJ: Princeton University Press, 2011)

Chapter 9: Globalization from a postcolonial perspective

Stanley Aronowitz and Heather Gautney, *Implicating Empire: Globalization and Resistance in the Twenty-first Century* (New York: Basic Books, 2003)

Michael Hardt and Antonio Negri, *Empire* (Cambridge, MA: Harvard University Press, 2000)

Naomi Klein, *Fences and Windows: Dispatches from the Frontlines of the Globalization Debate* (London: Flamingo, 2002)

John Madeley, *Big Business, Poor Peoples: The Impact of Transnational Corporations on the World's Poor* (London: Zed Books, 1999)

John Pilger, *The New Rulers of the World* (London: Verso, 2002)

Roberto Fernández Retamar, *Caliban and Other Essays*, trans. Edward Baker (Minneapolis: Minnesota University Press, 1989)

Ken Saro-Wiwa, *Genocide in Nigeria: The Ogoni Tragedy* (London: Saros International Publishers, 1992)

Robert J. C. Young, '"Dangerous and Wrong": Shell, Intervention, and the Politics of Transnational Companies', *Interventions: International Journal of Postcolonial Studies* 1.3 (1999), pp. 439–64

Chapter 10: Ecology and indigeneity

Saliha Belmessous, ed., *Native Claims: Indigenous Law against Empire, 1500–1920* (Oxford: Oxford University Press, 2014)

Dipesh Chakraborty, *The Crises of Civilization: Exploring Global and Planetary Histories* (New York: Oxford University Press, 2018)

Ken S. Coates, *A Global History of Indigenous Peoples: Struggle and Survival* (Basingstoke: Palgrave Macmillan, 2004)

Arne Næss, *Ecology of Wisdom* (London: Penguin, 2016)

Rob Nixon, *Slow Violence and the Environmentalism of the Poor* (Cambridge, MA: Harvard University Press, 2011)

Feminism and ecology

Narmada dam: http://www.narmada.org

The Greenbelt movement: http://www.greenbeltmovement.org/

Luiz C. Barbosa, *Guardians of the Brazilian Amazon Rainforest: Environmental Organizations and Development* (New York: Routledge, 2017)

Elizabeth Deloughrey, *Postcolonial Ecologies: Literatures of the Environment* (New York: Oxford University Press, 2011)

Mary Mellor, *Feminism and Ecology* (Cambridge: Polity Press, 1997)

Rigoberta Menchú, *I, Rigoberta Menchú: An Indian Woman in Guatemala*, ed. Elisabeth Burgos-Debray, trans. Ann Wright (London: Verso, 1984)

Vandana Shiva, in association with J. Bandyopadhyay et al., *Ecology and the Politics of Survival: Conflicts over Natural Resources in India* (New Delhi: Sage, 1991)

Thomas Weber, *Hugging the Trees: The Story of the Chipko Movement* (New Delhi: Viking, 1988)

Chapter 11: Translation

Susan Bassnett and Harish Trivedi, *Post-Colonial Translation: Theory and Practice* (London: Routledge, 1999)

Paulo Freire, *Pedagogy of the Oppressed*, trans. Myra Bergman Ramos (Harmondsworth: Penguin, 1972)

Index

For the benefit of digital users, indexed terms that span two pages (e.g., 52–53) may, on occasion, appear on only one of those pages.

A

Aboriginals 41–2, 61–2, 73, 77–8
abortions 110–12
Abuja Declaration 61–2
Achebe, Chinua 29–31
activism
  anti-colonial 4, 6, 33–4
  ecological 131–9
  gender identity 103–5
  in India 117
  political 114–17
  see also feminism
Adorno, Theodor 37
Afghanistan, refugees from 16
Africa
  Che Guevara in 121
  revolutionary 119
African-Americans
  cultural influences in
    USA 6, 78–80
  Great Migration 16–17
Agamben, Giorgio 17–18
Algeria
  Fanon in 144–8

raï 81–90
  wearing of the veil 96–7
al-Kailani, Rashid 'Ali (Iraqi Prime
    Minister) 57–8
al-Sa'id, Amina 108–9
Ambedkar, B. R. 47
Anderson, Benedict 67–70
anti-colonialists 4, 6, 33–4
Anzaldúa, Gloria 28, 37
apartheid 20
Arabic, mathematic and scientific
    knowledge 22
'Arab Woman' image 92–5
Arendt, Hannah 21
Aristotle 141
asylum seekers 14–15
  see also refugees
Atatürk, Kemal 95
Australia 77–8
  landlessness 61–2

B

Baghdad, Iraq 51–60
balance of power 6

Bandung Conference (1955) 20–2
Banksy 74
Battle of the Veil 95
Behn, Mira 131–2
Bentham, Jeremy 37
Bethlehem, Palestine 74
Bhabha, Homi K. 33–4, 79–80,
    85–6, 143
bilingualism 26
    in literature 28–9
Bishnoi community 133–5
black culture, influence in USA 6
Black Skin, White Masks
    (Fanon) 147
Blair, Tony (British Prime
    Minister) 59–60
Blida-Joinville psychiatric hospital,
    Algeria 145–8
Bohlman, Philip V. 81
Bolivia 122, 130–1
borders 66–7, 73–4
    around cities 73–6
    walls as 73–4
border thinking 37, 67
Boupacha, Djamila 110–12
Boyle, Danny 74
Brazil, landlessness 61
Brontë, Charlotte 29–30
Burundi 127–8

C

Cabral, Amilcar 22–3
Canada 66
Canclini, Néstor García 37
capitalism
    vs nomadism 64
    and slavery 42–3
Caribbean 144
caste system 45–8, 117
Castro, Fidel 120–1
Césaire, Aimé 29–30, 33–4, 37–9,
    79–80, 123–4
Chaman, Pakistan 13
Chatterjee, Partha 33–4

Che-Lumumba Club 119
Chipko movement, India 131–7
Choisir group 110–12
Churchill, Winston (British Prime
    Minister) 54–5, 58–9
cities, divided by walls 73–6
climate change 137–9
    see also ecology
Clinton, Bill (US President) 74–6
Coetzee, J. M. 29–30
Cold War, invention of 'third
    world' 20–1
collective movements,
    feminism 8–9
colonial discourse analysis 3
colonial feminism 106–7
colonization, types 32–3
Conrad, Joseph 30–1
Couto, Mia 29
Covid-19 crisis 101–2
creolization 144
Cuba 118–24
*Cuban Counterpoint: Tobacco and
    Sugar* (Ortiz) 80–1
cultural hybridity 78–90

D

Dalits 46–8
Dangarembga, Tsitsi 27
decerebralization 147–8
decoloniality 35–40
decolonization 4–7
    India 16–17
    intellectual 7, 33–4
Deleuze, Gilles and Félix
    Guattari 63–4
democracy 69
deterritorialization 63, 142–3
Devi, Amrita 133–5
Devi, Phoolan (Bandit
    Queen) 47, 116–17
Discourse on Colonialism
    (Césaire) 39
Djebar, Assia 24–5

double consciousness 44–5, 78–9
Du Bois, W. E. B. 44–5, 48, 78–9
Dussel, Enrique 37–8

E

ecology 129–39
economics, global South 6–7
education
    vs experience 18
    languages of 25–7
    postcolonial studies 34–5
    in a refugee camp 19
Egypt, wearing of the veil 92–5,
    100–2
El Guindi, Fadwa 99–100
English language 25–6
    and the caste system 47–8
Enlightenment 37
Ethiopia 125–6
Eurocentrism 2–3
Europe
    decoloniality 39
    empires 4–5
    'migrant crisis' 16
    migrants from 16–17
    nation-states 65–6
experience, vs education 18
exploitation colonies 32–4

F

facial recognition cameras, hiding
    from 101–2
Faisal II (King of Iraq) 54–5
Fanon, Frantz 4, 21, 27, 33–4,
    37–8, 146
    Black Skin, White Masks 147
    in Blida-Joinville psychiatric
        hospital 145–8
    on culture 79–80
    Front de libération nationale
        (FLN) 148–9
    on racism 43–5
    similarity to Che Guevara 122–4

on the veil 96–7, 102
    The Wretched of the Earth
        118–21, 129–30, 147–8
Fanon, Josie 121
feminism 8–9
    colonial 106–7
    and modernity 105–6
    against patriarchal
        nationalism 70–1
    'postcolonial' 110–12, 114–15
    post-independence 108–10
    as Western concept 105, 107–8
    see also activism; women
Flaubert, Gustave 2–3
Foucault, Michel 23, 37
France, banning of the veil 95
Friel, Brian 142–3
Front de libération nationale
    (FLN) 148–9
fusion 87

G

Gandhi, Leela 69–70
Gandhi, M. K. 4, 29, 105–6, 131
Gaza Strip 18–19
gender identity 103–4
Germany, migrants from 16–17
Ghosh, Amitav 30–1
Gilroy, Paul 43
Glissant, Édouard 29, 37,
    79–80, 144
globalization 77–8, 124–7,
    137–9
global South
    economics 6–7
    sexuality 104–5
    Tricontinental Conference
        (1966) 21–2
Gopal Ashram 132
Gramsci, Antonio 23–4
Greenbelt Movement, Kenya
    137–9
Guevara, Che 37–8, 118–24
Guha, Ranajit 23–4, 33–4

H

Haavara Agreement (1933) 16–17
Halimi, Gisèle 110–13
hashtags 39–40
Heart of Darkness (Conrad) 30–1
Herder, Johann Gottfried 68–9
Hinduism 46–8
Hindutva movement 69, 105–6
homelessness 64
homosexuality 103–5
Horkheimer, Max 37
humanitarian intervention 106–7
human rights, difficulties for
    refugees 16–17
Huntingdon, Samuel P. 4–5

I

identities
    double consciousness 44–5, 78–9
    gender 103–4
    and languages 27–8
    national 67–9
imagined communities 67–70
independence, limitations 5–6
India
    borders 66
    caste system 45–8, 117
    Chipko movement 131–7
    context for postcolonial
        theory 9
    cultural values 79–80
    decolonization 16–17
    Hindutva movement 69, 105–6
    landlessness 61
indigenous populations 33,
    129–31
    Latin America 37–8
    as nomads 62–4
Indonesia 71
inequality 4–7, 127–8
intellectual decolonization 7, 33–4
International Monetary Fund
    (IMF) 126–7

Iraq 51–60
Iraq Petroleum Company (IPC) 57
Islam
    and raï music 81, 84–5, 90
    veil 91
    women in 105, 109

J

Jalazone refugee camp,
    Palestine 18–19
Jalozai refugee camp, Pakistan 13–15
James, C. L. R. 37–8
Jane Eyre (Brontë) 29–30
Jeanson, Francis 122
Johannesburg, South Africa 20
Joyce, James 18

K

Kenya, Greenbelt Movement 137–9
Khaled, Cheb 86, 88–90
Khan Yunis refugee camp, Gaza
    Strip 18
Khatibi, Abdelkabir 28, 37
Kilito, Abdelfattah 29–30
knowledge
    alternative forms 22–3
    two types 18
Kurds 58–9
Kusch, Rodolfo 37–8

L

landlessness 61–2
    and nomadism 62–4
Landless Workers Movement
    (MST; Brazil) 61
languages 25–9
    and the caste system 47–8
    translation 140
Las Casas, Bartolomé de 37
Latin America 33
    Che Guevara in 122
    decoloniality 35–8

literature
  alternative perspectives 29–30
  cultural experiences in 30–1
  languages of 25–6, 28–9
  women in history 24–5
Locke, John 62–3
Lowe, Lisa 43
Lumumba, Patrice 119–20
Luxembourg 127–8

M

McLuhan, Marshall 124
Malcolm X 120–1
Maldonado-Torres, Nelson 35
Mao Zedong 23–4
Mariátegui, José Carlos 37–8
Marx, Karl 37, 41
Marxism 42–3
masks 97–9, 101–2, 147
Maspero, François 122
mathematics, origin 22
Memmi, Albert 28–9, 33–4
metaphor 141
Mexico 75
  border with USA 74–6
  landlessness 61
  wearing of the veil 97–9
Middle East, division of 51–60
Mignolo, Walter 35–8
migrants 16, 143–4
  historical 16–17
  see also refugees
modernity 105–8
Modisane, Bloke 20
Morales, Evo 130–1
Morrison, Toni 24–5
Moumié, Félix 122–3
multilingualism 26–7
  in literature 28–9
multinational companies 124–7
museums 39
music
  African-Americans 78–80
  raï 81–90

N

Naipaul, V. S. 16–17, 29–30
Narmada Bachao Andolan
  (NBA) 137–8
Nasraoui, Radhia 110–13
national identity 67–9
nationalism 69–71, 106
nation-states 64–6
  borders 66–7, 73–4
  depicted as female 70–1
  formation 16–17
  imagined communities 67–70
  inequality 127–8
  official languages 26–7, 65–6
  organization 6–7
Nazism 68–9
Négritude movement 79–80
neo-liberalism 6–7
Nervous Conditions
  (Dangarembga) 27
Nestlé company 125–7
Netherlands, creation 65–6
New York, USA, wearing of the
  veil 100–1
Ngũgĩ wa Thiong'o 7, 29–30
Nicosia 49–50
Nietzsche, Friedrich 141
Nigeria, Ogoni people 131
nomads 62–4
Non-Aligned Movement 20–1
North Africa
  Algerian raï music 81–90
  racism in 45

O

Obama, Barack (US President) 6
Ogoni people, Nigeria 131
Orangina company 144–5
orientalism 2–3
Orientalism: Western
  Representations of the Orient
  (Said) 2
Ortiz, Fernando 37–8, 80–1

Oslo Agreement (1993) 71–2
Ottoman Empire 52–3

P

Palestine 16–18
  fragmented 71–2
  landlessness 61–2
  walls as borders 74
Pankhurst, Sylvia 70–1
patriarchal system 8–9
  and modernity 105–6
  nationalism 70–1
  and the veil 91–2
Peace Review (1918) 55–6
Peshawar, Pakistan 12–15
Pinel, Philippe 145
place names 143
postcolonial feminism 110–12,
  114–15
postcolonialism
  as activism 6
  bottom-up perspective
    9–10
  original use of term 3
postcolonial politics 112–17
postcolonial studies 34–5
postcolonial theory
  development 9
  perspectives 10
poverty 127–8
Project Wizard 119–20

Q

Qatar 127–8
Qissa Khawani Bazaar,
  Peshawar 12–13
queering 103–5

R

racial capitalism 42–3
racial hierarchies 45–8

racial theory 41–2
  caste system 45–8
racism 43–5
Rafah refugee camp, Palestine
  18–19
raï (Algeria) 81–90
Raj Anand, Mulk 29–30
Rama, Angel 142–3
rebellions 5
refugees 12–16
  historical 16–17
  personhood 17–18
Remitti, Cheikha (Queen of
  Raï) 83–4, 88–90
resistance 5
  in Egypt 109
  against patriarchal
    nationalism 70–1
Retamar, Roberto
  Fernández 118–19
reterritorialization 63
'Rhodes Must Fall' movement 39
Rhys, Jean 29–30
Robinson, Cedric J. 42–3
Rodney, Walter 37–8
Roma (gypsies) 63–4
Roy, Arundhati 105–6
Royal Air Force (RAF) 52,
  54–6, 58–9
Rushdie, Salman 29–30, 79–80

S

Said, Edward W. 2–3, 9,
  33–6, 91–2
science, origin 22
Selvon, Sam 29–30
Senghor, Léopold 79–80
settler colonialism 33, 35, 62, 129
sexuality 103–5
Shell company 124–5
Shiva, Vandana 131–3, 136–7
slavery 41–3
  tobacco and sugar 80

Smith, Zadie 29–30
socialism 121
Sophiatown, South Africa 20
South Africa 20
    landlessness 61–2
South America, decoloniality 35
sovereignty, limitations 5–6
Soviet Union, collapse 6–7
Spanish America 33
Spivak, Gayatri C. 24–5, 33–4, 105
Spratly Islands, South
    China Sea 66
Sri Lanka 69
stereotyping 143
subaltern perspectives 4, 9–10
    origin of term 23–5
    political activism 115–17
    women 24–5
Subcomandante
    Marcos 37–8, 97–9
Sykes, Mark and François
    Georges-Picot 52–3
Syria, refugees from 16

T

Tagore, Rabindranath 70–1
territorialization 63
Things Fall Apart (Achebe)
    30–1
third way 21–2
'third world' 20–1
Tijuana, Mexico 74–6
trade routes 32
transculturation 80
translation 140–44
tree-hugging 133–5
Tricontinental Conference
    (1966) 21–2
Trump, Donald (US
    President) 6, 74–6
Tuareg people 99
Tunisia 110–12
Turkey 95

U

universities, decolonization
    34–5
USA
    African-American
        culture 6, 78–80
    border with Mexico 74–6
    cultural changes 6
    Great Migration of
        African-Americans 16–17
    inequality 6–7
    migrants 16–17
    national identity 67–9
    wearing of the veil 100–1

V

veil 91–102
Village in a Jungle, The
    (Woolf) 30–1

W

walls as borders 73–4
Walsh, Catherine 35
Wangari Maathai 137–9
Western view of the world 2–3
    cultural literature 30–1
    diversity of 109–10
    ecology 136–7
    feminism 105, 107–8
    forms of knowledge 22–3
    organization of
        nation-states 6–7
    veils 92–5, 100
Wide Sargasso Sea (Rhys)
    29–30
women
    changing cultural attitudes
        towards 8–9
    colonial feminism 106–7
    as depiction of nation-states 70–1
    ecological activism 131–9

women (*cont.*)
  in Islam 105, 109
  and modernity 106
  and postcolonial
    politics 114
  as subaltern activists 115–17
  subaltern perspectives 24–5
  wearing of the veil 91–102
  see also feminism
Woolf, Leonard 30–1
Woolf, Virginia 70–1

World Bank 126–7, 136–7
world powers 5
World Trade Organization
    (WTO) 126–7
Wretched of the Earth, The (Fanon)
    118–21, 129–30, 147–8

Z

Zapatista movement 61, 97–9
Zimbabwe, landlessness 61–2

Geopolitics
A Very Short Introduction
Klaus Dodds

In certain places such as Iraq or Lebanon, moving a few feet either side of a territorial boundary can be a matter of life or death, dramatically highlighting the connections between place and politics. For a country's location and size as well as its sovereignty and resources all affect how the people that live there understand and interact with the wider world. Using wide-ranging examples, from historical maps to James Bond films and the rhetoric of political leaders like Churchill and George W. Bush, this Very Short Introduction shows why, for a full understanding of contemporary global politics, it is not just smart - it is essential - to be geopolitical.

'Engrossing study of a complex topic.'

Mick Herron, Geographical.

CRITICAL THEORY
A Very Short Introduction
Stephen Eric Bronner

In its essence, Critical Theory is Western Marxist thought with the emphasis moved from the liberation of the working class to broader issues of individual agency. Critical Theory emerged in the 1920s from the work of the Frankfurt School, the circle of German-Jewish academics who sought to diagnose--and, if at all possible, cure--the ills of society, particularly fascism and capitalism. In this book, Stephen Eric Bronner provides sketches of famous and less famous representatives of the critical tradition (such as George Lukács and Ernst Bloch, Theodor Adorno and Walter Benjamin, Herbert Marcuse and Jurgen Habermas) as well as many of its seminal texts and empirical investigations.

www.oup.com/vsi

ECONOMICS
A Very Short Introduction
Partha Dasgupta

Economics has the capacity to offer us deep insights into some of the most formidable problems of life, and offer solutions to them too. Combining a global approach with examples from everyday life, Partha Dasgupta describes the lives of two children who live very different lives in different parts of the world: in the Mid-West USA and in Ethiopia. He compares the obstacles facing them, and the processes that shape their lives, their families, and their futures. He shows how economics uncovers these processes, finds explanations for them, and how it forms policies and solutions.

'An excellent introduction . . . presents mathematical and statistical findings in straightforward prose.'

Financial Times

www.oup.com/vsi

GLOBALIZATION
A Very Short Introduction
Manfred Steger

'Globalization' has become one of the defining buzzwords of our time - a term that describes a variety of accelerating economic, political, cultural, ideological, and environmental processes that are rapidly altering our experience of the world. It is by its nature a dynamic topic - and this *Very Short Introduction* has been fully updated for 2009, to include developments in global politics, the impact of terrorism, and environmental issues. Presenting globalization in accessible language as a multifaceted process encompassing global, regional, and local aspects of social life, Manfred B. Steger looks at its causes and effects, examines whether it is a new phenomenon, and explores the question of whether, ultimately, globalization is a good or a bad thing.

www.oup.com/vsi

INTERNATIONAL MIGRATION
A Very Short Introduction
Khalid Koser

Why has international migration become an issue of such intense public and political concern? How closely linked are migrants with terrorist organizations? What factors lie behind the dramatic increase in the number of women migrating? This *Very Short Introduction* examines the phenomenon of international human migration - both legal and illegal. Taking a global look at politics, economics, and globalization, the author presents the human side of topics such as asylum and refugees, human trafficking, migrant smuggling, development, and the international labour force.

www.oup.com/vsi

INTERNATIONAL RELATIONS
A Very Short Introduction
Paul Wilkinson

Of undoubtable relevance today, in a post-9-11 world of growing political tension and unease, this *Very Short Introduction* covers the topics essential to an understanding of modern international relations. Paul Wilkinson explains the theories and the practice that underlies the subject, and investigates issues ranging from foreign policy, arms control, and terrorism, to the environment and world poverty. He examines the role of organizations such as the United Nations and the European Union, as well as the influence of ethnic and religious movements and terrorist groups which also play a role in shaping the way states and governments interact. This up-to-date book is required reading for those seeking a new perspective to help untangle and decipher international events.

www.oup.com/vsi